Your Towns and Cities in the Gre

Frome
in the Great War

To the people of Frome
both past and present

Your Towns and Cities in the Great War

Frome
in the Great War

David Lassman

Pen & Sword
MILITARY

First published in Great Britain in 2016 by
PEN & SWORD MILITARY
an imprint of
Pen and Sword Books Ltd
47 Church Street
Barnsley
South Yorkshire S70 2AS

Copyright © David Lassman, 2016

ISBN 978 1 47383 593 1

Printed and bound in England
by CPI Group (UK) Ltd, Croydon, CR0 4YY

Typeset in Times New Roman by Chic Graphics

Pen & Sword Books Ltd incorporates the imprints of
Pen & Sword Archaeology, Atlas, Aviation, Battleground, Discovery,
Family History, History, Maritime, Military, Naval, Politics, Railways,
Select, Social History, Transport, True Crime, Claymore Press,
Frontline Books, Leo Cooper, Praetorian Press, Remember When,
Seaforth Publishing and Wharncliffe.

For a complete list of Pen and Sword titles please contact
Pen and Sword Books Limited
47 Church Street, Barnsley, South Yorkshire, S70 2AS, England
E-mail: enquiries@pen-and-sword.co.uk
Website: www.pen-and-sword.co.uk

Contents

Acknowledgements

Thanks to Diane Rouse, Michael McGarvie, Frome Library, Sue Bucklow, Brian Marshall, Frome Museum, Jane Wood, Mick Davis, Frome Film & Video Makers Club, Claire Wilson, *Frome Standard*, Nigel Lassman, John Payne, Frome Community Education, Will George, Frome Writers' Collective, Alastair MacLeay and Frome Society for Local Study.

Thanks also to the helpful and friendly team at Pen & Sword, including Roni Wilkinson, Irene Moore, Jon Wilkinson, Matt Jones, Jodie Butterwood and Lori Jones.

Every effort has been made to gain permissions for the reproduction of images and material in this book.

Foreword

I was delighted when David Lassman asked me to write a Foreword to this notable book on Frome in the Great War. David writes not only with ease and elegance but also with a passionate involvement in the unhappy period he is researching. He has dug deep into the records of a subject which has not been given much attention by historians. His research has been thorough and widespread and he has an eye for detail and even for humour.

Among his many sources have been the files of *The Somerset Standard* and *The Somerset & Wilts Journal*. Indeed, it is astonishing how much quite sensitive information in war time was allowed into the local newspapers. Some of the letters from the front are both poignant and illuminating. Inevitably David takes us frequently to the trenches year after terrible year telling of the experiences of local men: their lives, sometimes terrifying, at other times boring, their food, even their ablutions, their wounds and deaths. Many local soldiers became flesh and blood characters in David's words including two VCs.

Life at the front has dominated the history of the Great War. But it is astonishing how much David has discovered about what was going on in Frome as the years rolled by. Frome was a garrison town and resolute. As the war went on and the casualties mounted, grief became widespread and we hear of Frome's sombre Christmases. But the townspeople held their nerve, never ceased to support the war effort with blood and money, enduring with a stoic spirit. It would be hard to think of any subject David hasn't covered, the effect on schools, the conscientious objectors, the contribution of animals, the pressure on farmers and the growing involvement of women, to name but a few.

I read *Frome in the Great War* with pleasure and learnt much from it. I heartily recommend this outstanding book to you.

Michael McGarvie
President, Frome Society for Local Study

Introduction

The small market town of Frome is something of a paradox. It is located in Somerset, yet lies so far along the eastern end of the Mendip Hills, and away from the county's administrative centre of Taunton, it might as well be in Wiltshire, the neighbouring county it borders. The town has a history of religious dissent and non-conformity, yet owes its existence to a venerated man of the cloth who would later be canonised. Even pronouncing its name can give rise to confusion, as those unfamiliar with it inevitably try to rhyme it with home, rather than broom.

Throughout the centuries Frome has seen its fortunes fluctuate on numerous occasions, often bringing financial hardship to the town and

The market town of Frome, Somerset.

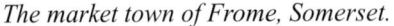

its population through its own apathy and resistance to change, yet time and time again it has reinvented itself and risen phoenix-like to further prosperity. One of the latest incarnations is its transformation from a town with a reputation as 'a bit of a dump', at the beginning of the twenty-first century, to being voted 'sixth coolest place to live in England' by *The Times* newspaper in 2013.

Through all of this, however, Frome has built a character and identity that, for the most part, is never changing. An identity which, as one columnist has noted 'seems to have revolved around the eminently sensible attitude of "To hell with national events! We will stay as we are."' And yet a hundred years ago, when called on by 'King and Country' to do its duty in the First World War, Frome rose to the task willingly and undertook it admirably. Men from Frome and the surrounding areas would see action in all theatres of war the global conflict encompassed and take part in the battles and campaigns, on land and at sea, which have become synonymous with this conflict: Ypres, Gallipoli, Jutland, and the Somme. At the same time, its civilian population would receive a special commendation after the war for their efforts throughout it.

The town's contribution did not stop there, however, as many of the returning soldiers and their families helped create several of the national and international monuments and memorials that would pay eternal tribute to their comrades who fell on the fields of Flanders and elsewhere.

Frome owes its existence to Saint Aldhelm, the Abbot of Malmesbury, who founded it towards the end of the seventh century. Legend has it that on a journey to Sherborne he forded a river with a steep incline on the other side. The area was surrounded by a great forest – Selwood – but halfway up the incline stood a clearing and here he decided to build a church dedicated to St John.

From then onwards, the newly-named settlement of Frome – from the Celtic word *ffraw* meaning fair and pertaining to the river running through it – seems to have thrived. Saxon kings used Frome as a base from which to hunt in

Saint Aldhelm, the founder of Frome.

Selwood Forest; it was the site of a Witenagemot – an assembly of important leaders in Anglo-Saxon times in 934; one of the first English kings, Eadred, died there in 955. It also appears in the Domesday Book.

Frome really came into its own though, from around the sixteenth century. Due to the huge number of sheep grazing in the area, along with its long established market and geographical location, the town became the centre of the East Somerset woollen industry and for a period of time was bigger – in terms of population and wealth – than its nearby neighbour Bath. In fact, when Daniel Defoe visited Frome in 1720, he remarked that the town had grown so much in the preceding decades that if it was to continue in the same manner it would, in a few years' time, 'very likely to be one of the greatest and wealthiest inland towns in England'.

Yet, barely a century later, when William Cobbett took in Frome during one of his 'rural rides', its once thriving textile industry had declined to such a point that,

[these] *'poor creatures at Frome have pawned all their things,*

The Market Place in Frome circa 1840. The view is looking up Bath Street, which had been completed about thirty years earlier and was named for Lord Bath of Longleat and not after the city.

or nearly all [and in the] *case of a man having two or three shirts, he is left with only one, and sometimes without any shirt; and, though this is a sort of manufacture that cannot very well come to a complete end; still it has received a blow from which it cannot possibly recover.'*

At the height of its textile production, however, it was said Frome was sending the equivalent of a wagon of cloth a day to London (each wagon containing 140 pieces). As the families owning the clothing businesses grew rich and powerful, so they built housing and developed facilities for their employees, expanding the centre outward in every direction. Yet as the industry developed its production methods, Frome seemed unable or unwilling to change with it and so as its northern rivals embraced modern mechanisation and reaped the rewards, the town found itself having to look elsewhere, to other industries, to restore its fortunes.

These other industries came in the form of firms such as Cockeys, originally a bell-foundry that grew into a major producer of components for the developing gas industry, J.W. Singer, a brass foundry and bronze-casting works, and Butler & Tanner, a print works that would eventually gain a world-wide reputation.

Along with the men whose firms were named after themselves, were also men of vision. One such person was Thomas Bunn, a financially independent solicitor whose life-time ambition became the reinvigoration of the town, so as to elevate it to its former position as being more important than Bath. (In the period of time Frome's textile industry had risen and fallen, this neighbouring city had foregone its own woollen industry – at least within its old medieval centre – and turned itself into the most fashionable health spa and tourist resort in England.) Bunn's ambitious plans included several crescents and a number of huge boulevards. In the end, only two Doric columns, today standing in Christchurch Street West, a number of public buildings and the aptly named Bath Street, came to fruition.

The beginning of the twentieth century saw the town struggling with its future once again. The number of poor had risen, unemployment was rife and by the summer of 1914, Frome, like everywhere else

The Market Place in Frome, in the years before the conflict that would change this town and the surrounding villages forever.

THE SOMERSET AND WILTS JOURNAL.

FROME FLOWER SHOW.

WET WEATHER SPOILS THE ATTENDANCE.

AN INCREASED ENTRY.

MUCH as the weather conditions prevailing interfered with the success of the function from the holiday-makers' point of view, the verdict of the horticulturist upon Frome Oddfellows' annual flower show on Monday, was that it was without qualification successful. There were more entries than last year—the total being 794 compared with 728, and never before had there been a higher level of quality throughout the classes.

There were remarkably few weak classes in the open-to-all section, and the very appearance of the tent was suggestive of the excellence of the exhibits. Fruit, flowers and vegetables, here, left nothing to be desired ; and the prizes were awarded on very close margins of superiority. Particularly good were the banks of flowering and foliage plants, a competition that has become more and more a feature of the show in recent years. For the first time for several shows Messrs. Cray, of Frome, were beaten for first place by Messrs. Tucker, of Trowbridge. There was very little between the exhibits, the beauty of which was effectively set off by the magnificent exhibition bank from Longleat that was erected under the experienced supervision of Mr. H. Gandy.

Much first class produce was staged in the cottagers' section. The vegetables made a bold

Rt. Hon. W. H. Long, M.P. Nine dessert apples : 1, W. H. Singer ; 2, Rt. Hon. W. H. Long, M.P. ; 3, J. Cray & Sons. Culinary ditto : 1, E. Fisher, Bath ; 2, H. Merritt, Larkhall, Bath ; 3, J. Cray & Sons. Twelve Plums : 1, Miss Harvey, Frome ; 2, W. B. Grist, Frome ; 3, Rt. Hon. W. H. Long, M.P. Six dishes of fruit grown in open air : 1, Rt. Hon. W. H. Long, M.P. ; 2, J. B. Lowe ; 3, A. G. Hayman. Melon : 1, Rt. Hon. W. H. Long, M.P. ; 2, A. G. Hayman ; 3, M. Hiles.

SPECIAL PRIZES.—*Given by Webb & Sons, Wordsley.* Six bunches sweet peas : 1, J. B. Lowe. Collection of vegetables, six kinds : 1, Rt. Hon. W. H. Long, M.P. ; 2, J. B. Lowe ; 3, A. J. Andrews, Batheaston.

Given by Sutton & Sons, Reading.—Collection vegetables, six kinds : 1, J. B. Lowe ; 2, A. F. Somerville ; 3, P. E. Warburton.

Given by Daniels Bros , Ltd , Norwich.—Collection vegetables, six kinds : 1, F. Dredge, Frome.

Given by Mr. A. Cray, Frome.—Six dahlias (amateurs and gentlemen's gardeners) : 1, E. Clarke ; 2, G. Clarke.

Vegetables, eight varieties : 1, Rt. Hon. W. H. Long, M.P. ; 2, Duchess of Somerset ; 3, J. B. Lowe ; 4, A. E. Trowbridge. Potatoes, ten varieties : 1, J. B. Lowe ; 2, A. F. Somerville ; 3, W. J. White, Timber Hill. Peas, 30 pods : 1, H. Green, Trowbridge ; 2, A. F. Somerville ; 3, W. J. White. Cucumbers : 1, A F. Somerville ; 2, J. Cray & Son ; 3, Duchess of Somerset. Onions : 1, J. B. Lowe ; 2, Miss Stukins ; 3, R. L. Taylor, Maiden Bradley (gardener, Mr. Robins). Tomatoes, eight pounds : 1, Somerset Fruit Co. ; 2, F. Ackland ; 3, J. Cray & Sons. Twelve tomatoes :

The Somerset and Wilts Journal's *report of the Annual Flower Show in Frome, which had been opened by Lady Bath. Little did its participants know what the week ahead held for them.*

throughout Europe, was under the clouds of a gathering storm, even if they were not fully aware of it. Certainly from the end of June, when Archduke Ferdinand was assassinated in Sarajevo, to the August Bank Holiday, when Germany declared war on France, the town seemed content to go about its own business much the same as normal. Indeed, on the same day as this latter event, the majority of Frome's population were no doubt more interested in the outcome of the various categories in the annual flower show than international affairs; a show that, despite the atrocious weather, drew a record number of entries and, according to the report in the *Somerset & Wilts Journal* published later that week, *'a higher than usual level throughout all classes'*. However, as the show's organisers, stall holders and competition entrants packed away and headed home that night, the lights were metaphorically going out all over Europe.

The following morning, Tuesday, 4 August 1914, Frome, along with the rest of the country, found itself at war. A way of life was over and things would never be the same again for this small market town.

CHAPTER 1

Eager for the Fight (Aug–Sept 1914)

On Wednesday, 5 August 1914, Frome woke up to the reality of war. If the events happening in Europe over the bank holiday weekend and the declaration of war by Britain the previous day had seemed dream-like, then the mobilisation notices received by many of the town's male population were a rude awakening.

In and around the centre of Frome, as well as in the villages that lay on the outskirts, men made their preparations to leave and rejoin their regiments. These were mainly reservists, those who had previously served in the army but had since returned to civilian life, or else civilians who trained with the regular army and could be called up in the event of war.

From our modern-day perspective it is perhaps hard to imagine the euphoria and sense of eager anticipation that accompanied the men as they set off across the country to rejoin their regiments. There was, of course, the belief that even though the conflict might be bloody, it would be brief and over by Christmas. Therefore, as the men made their way to where their regiments were stationed, there was a real sense of not wanting to miss out on what was seen as being a great adventure, while at the same time serving King and Country.

The following years, with their trench warfare, chemical weapons, mass slaughter and all the other horrors now associated with the First

No. 191   Army Form D. 463A.

ARMY RESERVE.

GENERAL MOBILIZATION.

Notice to join the Army for Permanent Service.

Name _J. Fry_   Rank _L/Sgt_

Regimental } 7267   _Coldstream Guards._   { Regt. or
Number   }   { Corps.

You are hereby required to join the _Coldstream Guards._

at CHELSEA BARRACKS, LONDON.   on   **5 - AUG. 1914**

Should you not present yourself on that day, you will be liable to be proceeded against.

You will bring with you your "Small Book," your Life Certificate, Identity Certificate, and, if a Regular Reservist, Parchment Reserve Certificate.

Instructions for obtaining the sum of 3s. as an advance of pay and a Travelling Warrant where necessary, are contained in your Identity Certificate.

If your Identity Certificate is not in your possession and you are unable to proceed to join, you must report at once to this office, either personally or by letter.

Stamp of Officer i/c Records.

Numerous reservists from Frome and the surrounding area received mobilization notices, bringing home the reality of the situation the country as a whole now found itself in.

World War, would test (and in many cases shatter) this patriotism. This was especially true for the men – some no older than boys – who returned to Frome and outlying villages either physically or mentally scarred, or their relatives who were regrettably informed of a loved one's death. On that Wednesday morning in August 1914, however, this was another world away.

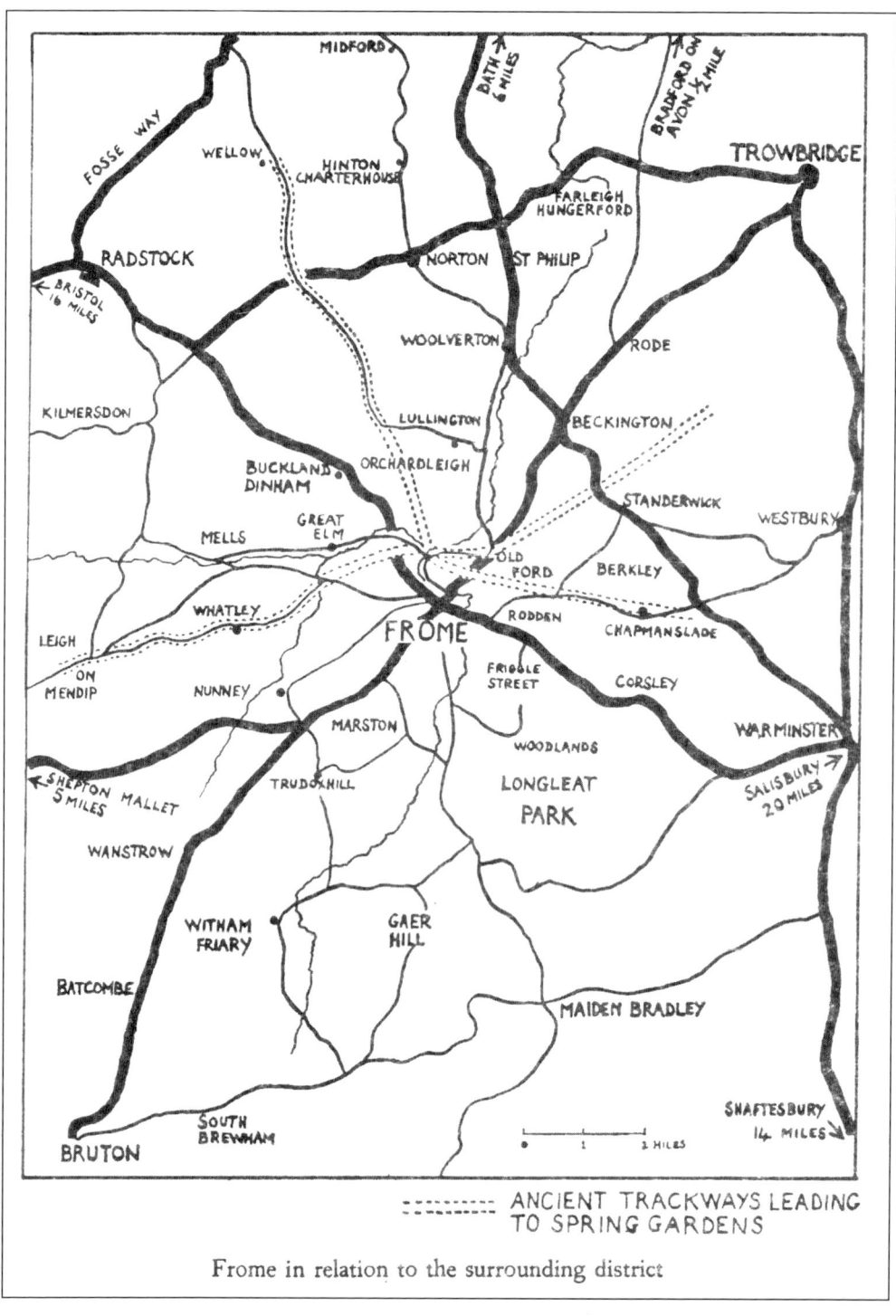

FOSSE WAY

MIDFORD

BATH 6 MILES

BRADFORD ON AVON ½ MILE

TROWBRIDGE

WELLOW

HINTON CHARTERHOUSE

FARLEIGH HUNGERFORD

RADSTOCK

NORTON ST PHILIP

BRISTOL 16 MILES

WOOLVERTON

RODE

KILMERSDON

LULLINGTON

BECKINGTON

BUCKLAND DINHAM

ORCHARDLEIGH

STANDERWICK

WESTBURY

MELLS

GREAT ELM

OLD FORD

BERKLEY

WHATLEY

FROME

RODDEN

CHAPMANSLADE

LEIGH ON MENDIP

NUNNEY

FRIGGLE STREET

CORSLEY

WARMINSTER

MARSTON

WOODLANDS

SHEPTON MALLET 5 MILES

TRUDOXHILL

LONGLEAT PARK

SALISBURY 20 MILES

WANSTROW

WITHAM FRIARY

GAER HILL

BATCOMBE

MAIDEN BRADLEY

SHAFTESBURY 14 MILES

SOUTH BREWHAM

1   2 MILES

BRUTON

- - - - - - - ANCIENT TRACKWAYS LEADING TO SPRING GARDENS

Frome in relation to the surrounding district

Frome and its relation to the surrounding villages and districts.

For many households in the Frome area, several members would be involved in the fighting during the coming weeks and months. Under the heading FROME FIGHTING FAMILIES, the *Somerset & Wilts Journal* listed those who had *'contributed heavily in sons and husbands to Great Britain's fighting forces'*. They included the Davages of Trinity Street, who, it was reported, had three sons in the forces, as did the Topps from Goulds Ground. Heading the list, however, was the Portch family, of Bath Road, Beckington, who had five of their six sons in the Royal Navy – the youngest son having only just left school – along with a son-in-law in the army.

Once the men returning to their regiments were waved off from Frome railway station by family, friends and onlookers, the following period of time for all the reservists travelling around the country became relatively typical. After rejoining their assigned units, they would undergo training and then make their way, in most cases, to embarkation points in order to cross the English Channel to France. Many Frome men belonged to the so called 'county' regiments and while some left England relatively quickly – the Wiltshires and Gloucesters went across within ten days of mobilisation, for example – others, such as the Somersets, would have to wait until later in the month.

If Frome had a 'home' regiment in the regular army, then it was the Somersets, named after the county in which the town was located, or Prince Albert's (Somerset Light Infantry) to give its full title. It had

Your King and Country Need You.

A CALL TO ARMS.

An addition of 100,000 men to his Majesty's Regular Army is immediately necessary in the present grave National Emergency.

Lord Kitchener is confident that this appeal will be at once responded to by all those who have the safety of our Empire at heart.

TERMS OF SERVICE.

General Service for a period of 3 years or until the war is concluded.

Age of Enlistment between 19 and 30.

HOW TO JOIN.

Full information can be obtained at any Post Office in the Kingdom or at any Military depot.

GOD SAVE THE KING!

One of the first newspaper advertisements calling for volunteers. It would have been seen by men in Frome and struck a chord with the majority of them.

After the reservists had rejoined their regiments, they underwent physical fitness training to get them back into shape.

been formed in 1685, when James II expanded the size of the army in order to quash the Monmouth Rebellion. Originally called the Earl of Huntingdon's Regiment of Foot, after the man tasked with raising it, the regiment changed its name and acquired its county moniker in 1782, as did several other regiments, in a bid to aid local recruiting. Its royal patronage was added in 1842 and after several slight name alterations throughout the rest of the nineteenth and early twentieth centuries, finally became known as Prince Albert's (Somerset Light Infantry) in 1912.

Lord Kitchener's famous recruiting poster, although at the time it was only one of many that was used in an attempt to persuade the men of Frome and elsewhere to enlist.

The majority of reservists began to arrive at their mustering points with 'creditable punctuality' in the days following mobilisation and by 8 August 1914 the 1st Battalion of the Somerset Light Infantry (1/Somersets) 'was assembled and awaiting orders' at its base at Colchester. The battalion's peacetime number was between 600-700 men but by the time they were ready to leave for France, their number had swelled to 1,000. A week or so later they left their base for Harrow School, encamping on its playing fields and taking part in further training. Four days later, on 21 August 1914, they entrained for Southampton and the ship that would take them across to the front line.

As soon as the war began the call for men went out. Captain Russell Tanner, a recruiting officer for D Company, 2nd Battalion Somerset National Reserve, made an appeal in the *Somerset & Wilts Journal*. The response was immediate and in the following week's paper, the *Journal* could report that nearly fifty men had answered the appeal and that D Company's strength now stood at 200. In addition, an emergency corps – based in Frome and whose role was to undertake local duties – had been raised and consisted of 100 men. Within a fortnight, Frome District Emergency Corps, or Tanner's Own, as it became known, stood at 250 men. They met nightly at Keyford Drill Hill, which had been built earlier in the year and stood up the hill from Bath Street, where they undertook drilling and various training in preparation for any eventuality.

Recruiting for the regular army in Frome, however, was initially more difficult. This was due to the absence of a permanent recruiting officer in the town. This was quickly rectified by a travelling recruiting office, a makeshift solution created by Field Marshal Lord Kitchener in order to raise the 100,000 men required for his second army, which

The Drill Hall in Keyford, Frome, which had only opened in February 1914.

The old Market Hall as it looks today, which is now known as the Cheese & Grain.

was to reinforce the British Expeditionary Force already in France. The travelling office resulted in several Frome men joining the Grenadier Guards after one of their recruiting officers visited the town.

The stopgap solution of a travelling recruiting office was swiftly followed by a public meeting on the following Tuesday, held at the town's Market Hall (known today as the Cheese & Grain). The meeting was presided over by Lord Bath, whose residence was the nearby Longleat Estate. During the evening he gave a rousing speech to the packed hall, in which he said that knowing the neighbourhood as he did, he was convinced the men of Somerset – and Frome in particular – would not be behind in coming forward to serve their country at the gravest time of need since the Napoleonic Wars. By the end of the meeting the Somerset Light Infantry saw their numbers swelled by thirty men and a permanent recruiting officer – a Sergeant Deeming – was appointed for the Frome district.

Once the men who had enrolled at the Market Hall meeting left for their 'new' regiment, their induction followed similar lines to all the other thousands upon thousands of volunteers elsewhere around the country. After first being assigned an army number and 'kitted out', the recruits underwent basic training, which included learning how to drill, route marching and instruction on how to use weapons. During this period of their enlistment the men usually belonged to a training unit especially created for the purpose. In the case of the Somerset Light Infantry, it was the 3rd (Special Reserve) Battalion, based at Devonport. Once this training had been completed, they would join their chosen regiment proper and in the majority of cases, make the journey across to France.

At the start of the war those volunteering could more or less choose which regiment they wanted to join. For many local men this was usually their county regiment, as the thirty men at the Market Hall

On enlisting, men from Frome and the surrounding area would take the oath to serve King and Country.

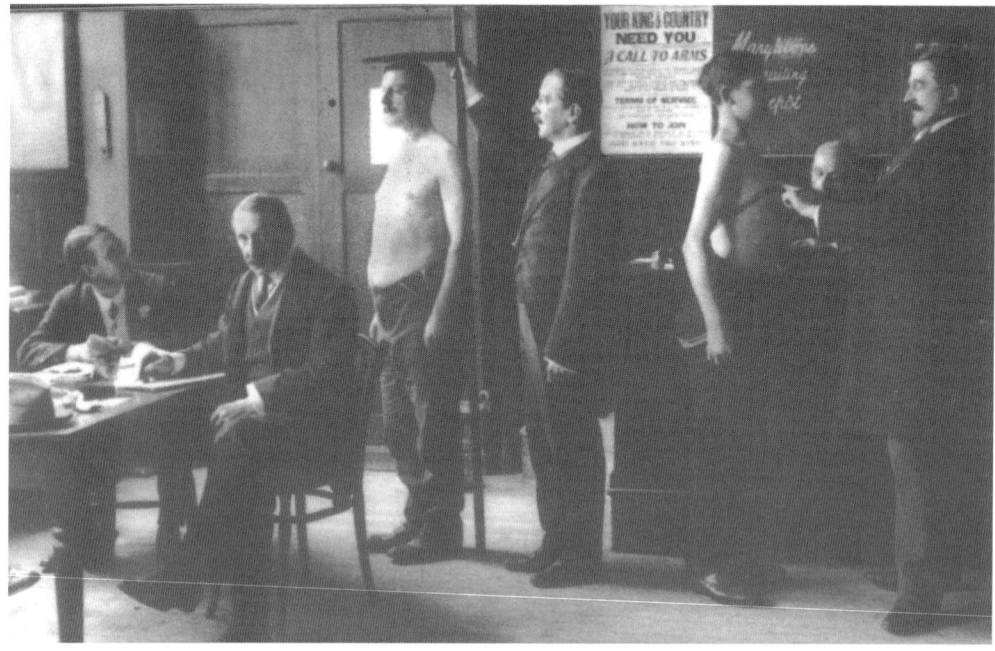

As part of the induction process new recruits from Frome would be given medicals.

Along with drilling and route marching, new recruits were trained in the use of weapons.

meeting had done, although there were other options and many Frome men joined those regiments instead. These included the Guards: Coldstream and Grenadiers; the cavalry: Dragoons, Hussars or Lancers; or any number of supporting and specialist units, such as the Royal Field Artillery or the Royal Engineers.

Whatever regiment or unit a volunteer ended up in and once basic training had been completed, he would then be assigned to a particular battalion in the regiment. This battalion would normally consist of around 1,000 men. With so many wanting to join up in the first months of the war – 750,000 by the end of September 1914, and then on average another 125,000 per month – several extra battalions had to be quickly created. Each battalion would be made up of several platoons, which in turn comprised companies and then within those, sections. The battalion itself, however, was a relatively small combat unit and so many were drawn together from the various regiments, along with artillery and supporting units, to form a brigade. These brigades were then combined to form a division, which in turn were organised into corps. Finally, these corps would form an army. The men who went to France in August 1914 as part of the British Expeditionary Force belonged to one of the three corps that made up the BEF, or else were part of the ancillary forces accompanying it.

As all the above was happening with the armed forces, Frome was beginning to settle down to being a town at war and the reality of what this meant for the local population. The edition of the *Somerset & Wilts Journal* published on the Friday after war was declared, attempted to dictate the mood the town should adopt:

> *'As far as we can see, force being the predominant factor in civilisation, this war after a certain point became inevitable. Nothing remains for this nation but to face it with fortitude and courage, and to use every means to shorten its course and lessen the hardship that is sure to follow.'*

As if to reinforce this altered reality the town found itself now having to face, the *Journal* published not only a report of the flower show, which had been held the previous Bank Holiday Monday, but also a

After crossing the English Channel many men from Frome disembarked at Boulogne.

list of forthcoming agriculture and floral events that had been cancelled due to the conflict. These included flower shows at Leigh-on-Mendip and Chapmanslade, as well as the annual Frome District Agricultural Show, due to be held in September.

The newspaper also warned its readers against panic buying and gave advice as to the best ways of preventing it. This 'advice' had to be heeded, they argued, as panic buying would surely bring about premature scarcity and so assist the enemy. But seemingly this warning was already too late, as the newspaper also reported that stockpiling had begun in the town the previous Saturday. No doubt spurred on by the rumours of impending conflict that were circulating around town, many people had begun to buy large quantities of food to stockpile, causing prices to rise rapidly; the price of a pound of sugar, for example, had doubled within less than a week. Many grocers and provision dealers did their best to address the situation, by not fulfilling orders to their limit, but this merely caused resentment and buying elsewhere. On the other hand, many shopkeepers were accused of creating the situation by falsely inflating prices out of greed. The *Somerset Standard*, rival to the *Journal*, however, actually told a different story. According to them, things did not seem to be amiss, its readers being informed that:

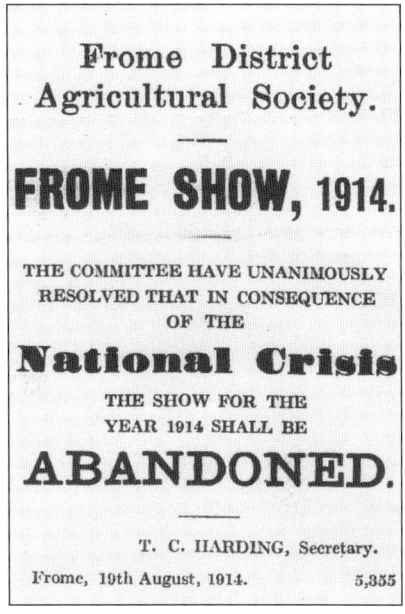

Frome District Agricultural Society.

FROME SHOW, 1914.

THE COMMITTEE HAVE UNANIMOUSLY RESOLVED THAT IN CONSEQUENCE OF THE

National Crisis

THE SHOW FOR THE YEAR 1914 SHALL BE

ABANDONED.

T. C. HARDING, Secretary.

Frome, 19th August, 1914.   5,355

A notice in a Frome newspaper announced the cancellation of the annual Agricultural Show, due to take place the following month. It was just one of many shows to suffer the same fate.

Although many shopkeepers felt they had no choice but to raise prices, some were accused of doing so out of pure greed.

'although there has been no great rush on the grocers and provision dealers in Frome during the week in anticipation of the rise in prices, they have been unusually busy but the orders have not forced the prices up unreasonably.'

As many employers began losing their workforce to the armed forces and the future of certain orders and contracts were in the balance – these mainly being overseas ones – firms began to cut their hours. The printing firm, Butler & Tanner, for example, initially reduced their working day by two hours, one in the morning and one in the evening, while J.W. Singer's foundry cut their total weekly hours from fifty-three to thirty-five. In spite of these reductions in hours, many employers suggested they would support the families of those workers who had gone off to do their duty. One business that actually increased its hours was Frome Post Office, staying open night and day for telegraphic purposes.

It was not just men employers began to lose to the service of King and Country though. As soon as war was declared, horses began to be

Dreadnought! Not the battleship but a type of printing press used by Butler and Tanner, and seen here at their Selwood premises.

Swapping English for French fields. A horse and plough engage in their customary work.

requisitioned from farms and businesses in the area, as well as from private individuals. The day the reservists left Frome to rejoin their regiments was a Wednesday – traditionally market day in the town – and this fact had not gone unnoticed by the army. Indeed, numerous farmers who had made the journey by horse, from around the region to the market place, had to find other means of getting home after their mode of transport was purchased for active service. Many of the horses were immediately sent to regiments preparing to go to France, which no doubt included the Somersets.

On Saturday, 22 August 1914, around eight-thirty in the morning, 1/Somersets finally set out from Southampton to cross the English Channel. As the coastline began to disappear they were given two pieces of paper. The first was from the King himself, entitled 'Message to the Troops'. It began *'You are leaving home to fight for the safety and honour of the Empire.'* George V then went on to inform them that he would be following their every movement with deepest interest and their welfare would never be absent from his thoughts. The second letter, from the British Army's Commander-in-Chief, Field Marshal Lord Kitchener, was more of a rallying call for each man to do his duty

Frome railway station where Private Russell worked as a goods porter before the war.

and perform the task at hand to the best of his ability, while simultaneously conducting himself with all the hallmarks of a British soldier. It ended with the words: *'Do your duty bravely. Fear God. Honour the King.'*

The journey across took all day and, due to an unsuitable tide, it was nearly midnight before the 1/Somersets finally set foot on French soil at Le Havre. After being given a rousing welcome by the locals, they made camp about six miles inland from the port. The following day they received orders to join the British Expeditionary Force, across the border in Belgium, engaged in what became known as the Battle of Mons.

The 1st Battalion of the Gloucestershire Regiment (1/Gloucesters) had already been in France for ten days by the time 1/Somersets landed and were now in the thick of the fighting. Vivid details of the battle later appeared in the *Somerset & Wilts Journal*, taken from an account by a Frome man wounded during it. Prior to the war, Private John Russell had been a goods porter at Frome Railway Station, but as he had previously served with the Gloucesters, he was called up at the start of hostilities. After landing in France, 1/Gloucesters eventually arrived at the town of Mons. Once there, they were immediately sent to the trenches:

'They had scarcely realised how close were the enemy to them before they were engaged in fighting of the most desperate

character. Exactly how desperate may be gauged from the circumstances in which Pte. Russell came to be among the wounded. His regiment was ordered to cover the movement of British artillery to a new position. They were given to understand that the enemy were comparatively distant. Suddenly, however, and without the slightest warning a withering hail of lead was poured on to the force – rifle and machine-gun fire from a body of Germans concealed not fifty yards away. The artillery horses stamped madly through the ranks of the Glosters. Pte. Russell caught between the gun carriages, rocking and swaying over the broken ground, went down with a bruised spine – which will probably render him unfit for further service. He managed to crawl for some yards on his hands and knees, seeking cover from the enemy's fire. His comrades fell back and Pte. Russell owes the fact that he is not "among the missing" to one of the little unrecorded acts of heroism which redeem the battlefield. "A couple of my chums," he said, "saw the fix I was in and came back for me. The bullets were whistling round them all the time, but they kept by me and between them carried me away to a ditch."'

Troops taking a break on the Western Front. The conflict would soon become stalemate.

Although the Battle of Mons had been a British success – the German advance having been brought to a halt – with the French in retreat to the south and the possibility of the BEF being outflanked, there seemed no other option than to retreat themselves.

The first action the 1/Somersets were involved in took place south-east of the French town of Solesmes, on 25 August 1914. As part of 11 Infantry Brigade, they were ordered on to high ground to help cover the retreat of II Corps from Mons. The following day, with the mission accomplished, they then formed part of a rearguard at the village of Ligny. On their right flank, dug in at the town of Caudry, was the 1st Battalion (Duke of Edinburgh's) Wiltshire Regiment. Along with the 1/Gloucesters, the Wiltshires arrived in France on 13 August and took part in the Battle of Mons. But now, like their neighbouring county regiment the Somersets, they were tasked with forming part of the rearguard in order to give the rest of the Expeditionary Force time to withdraw safely.

Both regiments engaged the Germans and held them back for as long as possible, but as the enemy advanced the two regiments came under heavy fire. This became known as the Battle of Le Cateau and it was during this encounter the first fatalities from the Frome area occurred, both men belonging to the Somersets. Private Ernest William Davidge was only 18 years old when he was killed on 26 August 1914, yet he had been serving in 1/Somersets for almost a year. He was born at Tytherington, but at the time of his death his mother lived at Feltham Hill in Frome. Also killed in action on the same day was Private Bertram Henry Vincent, whose family lived in Rode, near Frome. Despite holding the Germans at bay throughout the day, at five o'clock in the afternoon, orders came for both the Somersets and the Wiltshires, as part of their respective Infantry Brigades, to retreat once more.

Private Bertram Vincent was one of the first to be killed, on 26 August 1914.

Throughout the rest of August and into September, what is now known as the Retreat from Mons took place and with it came more deaths of men from Frome and the surrounding villages. These included Privates Albert Hillier and Harold Bull, both from 1/Wiltshires – the latter leaving a widow and new born baby – Mells resident Sergeant Thomas King of the Coldsteam Guards and George Woods from Rode, who was a driver with the 56th Battery Royal Field Artillery.

Private Harold Bull died on 14 September 1914, leaving behind a widow and young baby.

As the deaths of local men began to mount up, the stark reality of what those still in France were involved in began to seep back to Frome and elsewhere. This was mainly through letters soldiers wrote to their family and friends, many of which were printed verbatim in the local newspapers, or else through first hand accounts by the wounded, such as Private Russell and others, now convalescing back in England.

With so many of the original soldiers of the British Expeditionary Force now killed or wounded, the volunteers who had enlisted since the outbreak of war were now being sent out to replace them. And if they still did not know exactly what to expect on reaching the front lines, at least they could identify the enemy once they got there. For those left behind, who were also engaged in their own 'war', it was much more difficult. This was because the enemy they were fighting wore no identifying uniforms, no distinguishing markings or even

Egford Reservoir under construction in 1879. It was opened the following year and became an obvious target for saboteurs during the First World War.

possessed any visible weapons. This 'enemy' was, for the most part, unseen and unknown, deliberately engaged in doing all they could to blend into the background.

Although rumours of German spies on British soil had been rife in the pre-war years – mainly through books such as Ernest Childers' novel *The Riddle of the Sands*, which told the tale of a British yachtsman stumbling across a German plot to invade England – it was, for the most part, pure imagination and fear-mongering. Once the hostilities began, however, it became reality. Therefore, throughout the villages, towns and cities, as well as in the countryside, the British people were told they had to be on guard against German spies and acts of espionage. In the Frome area local civilian forces and boys' organisations were tasked with guarding positions of importance. Boy Scouts were posted at the reservoir at Egford, in Frome, while Somerset Naval Cadets stood watch at the ones at Downhead and Leigh-on-Mendip.

At the same time, the government introduced various Defence of the Realm Acts – or DORAs as they became known – one of which concerned the censoring of all outward-bound overseas mail, in order to stop potential communication with the enemy. The provisions of the Act and subsequent additions gave the government unprecedented power over all aspects of British life; some people might say it has never been truly relinquished since. These included punishable offences such as suspicious conduct, the giving of information, the spreading of false reports or inciting to mutiny, sedition or disaffection. Any British subject or alien could be prosecuted for infringing the act or in anyway endangering the state.

The result of all this 'spy talk' and potentially draconian measures was to create a sense of paranoia and suspicion of anyone 'foreign', whether through their nationality or merely the person being a stranger. Anyone unknown coming into the Frome district would immediately be viewed with suspicion and observed accordingly. Although there were no doubt successes, there were also many potentially embarrassing situations which, in some cases, became almost farcical. One incident in Frome took place near the reservoir at Cottle's Oak, Broadway, where a man was briefly arrested for allegedly poisoning

Local Frome Scout Troops were given the responsibility of guarding potentially vulnerable locations, such as reservoirs, against saboteurs and spies.

the water supply and sketching the reservoir. The boy scouts on duty informed the police as to what they had seen, but when an officer went to question the person, the 'sketch' book was found to actually be less incriminating. The man, a *'quite reputable working man'* according to the *Journal*, was merely waiting for a friend and to pass the time took out a time-sheet to do some calculations. He was quickly released.

Another potentially embarrassing situation, concerning a reputable person briefly coming under suspicion, also appeared in the *Journal*. Although in this case the newspaper put a positive spin on the incident:

> *'The boy scouts on guard at Frome water supply reservoir are carrying out their duties with a thoroughness which does credit to their corps. The latest evidence of their zeal is afforded by an adventure which befell Mr E. Tylee, of Chantry, a well-known member of the Frome Board of Guardians.'*

On his way to a meeting of the Guardians on his bicycle, Mr Tylee had dismounted at the top of Egford hill and sat on the roadside. Here, he took out a pocket-book and began writing. The watchful scouts sought assistance from a council employee, also guarding the water supply. Armed with a club, the council employee approached Mr Tylee who, obviously startled, tried to remount his bicycle. A brief struggle ensued, followed by an interrogation. Thankfully for Mr Tylee, as the newspaper reported, he was able to prove who he was and his reason for being there and so the incident was resolved.

It was not only on the ground where potential threats could materialise. In mid-August, for example, the *Somerset & Wilts Journal* reported the sighting of an 'airship' over Badcox. A bright light in the sky had caused concern in the vicinity and a crowd to gather. Telescopes and field glasses were brought to observe what was believed to be a German airship – otherwise known as the dreaded Zeppelin. When these were turned skyward, one observer claimed he could distinguish moving objects on board. It became a little more disconcerting when a sergeant in the Territorial Army went home for his rifle, intent on discharging it at the object, but in the end, however, he was dissuaded and by midnight the crowd had obviously seen enough and dispersed. As the *Journal* later reported it, the light was still there, although it turned out to be *'a bright but otherwise blameless star'*.

More serious, however, was an incident which occurred elsewhere in Frome. A 'mysterious foreigner' with a pocket camera was seen by several locals acting suspiciously near the railway bridges at Wallbridge. On completing his 'mission', the man apparently went to the nearby Railway Hotel, where he ordered a drink in broken English, before being spotted once more on the footpath to Willow Vale, the winding meadow area which runs alongside the River Frome. Here, the witness who saw him described the person as 'short in statue and of the military carriage'. The 'foreigner' then asked some boys about the footpath and where it led. After this, he was not seen again. The local police were called out, but, apart from briefly questioning what turned out to be a bona fide visitor, their investigations led nowhere and they were left empty-handed. The fact there had been someone acting suspiciously, asking questions and taking photographs was seemingly not in doubt and it was a reminder to the readers of the *Journal* and the rest of the local populace that vigilance needed to be retained at all times.

If strangers coming into Frome were treated suspiciously though, then locals going outside the area needed to be equally aware of how their presence might be interpreted, as they were now in danger of being the 'stranger' themselves. One Frome person who did not heed this warning was the Reverend Johnson, Vicar of Holy Trinity Church. On a trip to Weymouth with his brother, the two men were stopped and arrested for being spies. With no suitable identification forthcoming, both men were taken to the local police station, where they were held until their identities could be proved. Discharged, they then went on their way. In many ways, they were the lucky ones, as there were also reports of incidents in which 'perfectly respected people' were shot at and wounded when not answering the challenge of sentries.

As dangerous as it might be back home, it was still a lot safer than in potential areas of conflict, like the North Sea, as was proved near the end of September. It was at this time that Frome suffered its first naval fatality. This was Able Seaman William Turner, aged 49, serving on HMS *Cressy*. The ship was part of a trio of British armoured cruisers patrolling the North Sea in order to protect British convoys; the other two cruisers were HMS *Aboukir* and HMS *Hogue*. On 22 September

HMS Cressy. *Along with HMS* Aboukir *and HMS* Hogue, *this armoured cruiser was sunk by a lone German U-boat in September 1914. Able Seaman William Turner was aboard and killed.*

1914, there was an explosion on one side of HMS *Aboukir* and she began to sink. HMS *Hogue* went to help but she too suffered an explosion. It was initially believed the two ships had hit mines, but by the time the *Cressy* was rescuing men from both ships, it was apparent they had been torpedoed by a nearby German U-boat. The *Cressy* became its third victim, sent to the bottom of the sea taking with it 25 officers and 536 men, including Able Seaman Turner.

Back on the Western Front, the British Retreat from Mons had been halted at the River Marne and slowly the Germans were pushed back to a defensive line along the River Aisne. With their advance halted, the German high command turned their attention to a coastal area between the Belgium and French border. Here, in the region known as Flanders, the two sides became embroiled in what became known as the Race to the Sea. Germany's objective was to gain the ports of Dunkirk, Calais and Boulogne, while extending their front line all the way to the Channel coast. The British, on the other hand, found themselves desperately trying to hold back the Germans around the coastal strip of the River Yser and the inland town of Ypres.

Those involved did not know it yet, but this was the beginning of what would be another four years of fighting, during which time this provincial town would endure three major battles around its confines and, by the end of the third one, be completely destroyed. Ypres would come to epitomise the sheer destructiveness of the war and its futility, a war which, although no buildings would be destroyed by enemy shells or streets occupied by foreign armies, would no less affect the people of Frome.

CHAPTER 2

Reality Sets In (Oct–Dec 1914)

When the war started, at the beginning of August 1914, several Frome people found themselves in the unenviable position of being stuck on the continent and were either unable to get home straight away or else experienced great difficulty in doing so. The Vicar of Frome, William Randolph, and his wife, for example, had been holidaying in Switzerland and although they managed to get back to Frome relatively quickly, it was without their luggage. The same fate befell Lady Barlow, the wife of Frome's MP, who was actually in Germany attending a Church conference at the time of Britain's war declaration. Like the Randolphs, she and her party were faced with difficulties on their return journey – mainly in France, due to the mobilisation of their army and the commandeering of the railways – but overcame them to reach home safely – albeit also minus their luggage.

Neither of the above journeys, however, compared to the one experienced by Walter Case. The Frome businessman had gone to Carlsbad, within the Austro-Hungarian Empire, for his health. Once war was declared, Walter Case was unable to gain access to any money and, with the British Ambassador having already left, was stranded. According to reports in the Frome newspapers, he had been able to wire friends to tell them of his predicament, but they had heard nothing from him since then. Luckily for Walter, the American Consul was still

in the country and helped him to get across to Switzerland. From there
he made his way across France, first to Marseilles and then Paris, which
was now dangerously close to the front lines. From Paris, Walter finally
made it back to England, arriving in Frome mid-September, more than
six weeks after the hostilities had broken out. That wasn't the end of
his troubles, however, because on his return he found that fifty of his
workers at the tanneries he owned had enlisted.

THE NATIONAL HERB-GROWING ASSOCIATION.

A meeting was held in the Keyford Red
Cross Hospital, Frome, on Saturday last, to
further the work of the above association by
establishing, if possible, a branch in Frome.
The Countess Cairns presided over a fairly
good attendance. Lady Kathleen Thynne
acted as secretary. The following ladies and
gentlemen were present: The Rev. E. D.
Lear, Misses Crockford, Goodbourn, Pile,
Allwood, Macey, B. Hamblin, M. Baily,
Wingrove, Morris, Wall, Jenkins, Walwyn,
Bomford, Messrs. H. G. Chislett, Glover, C.
Mann, J. Morgan and Young.

The Chairman explained the object of the
meeting—to encourage the growing and collecting of herbs for medicinal and other
purposes, and thus become independent of the
markets of Central Europe.

The Herb Growing Association was one of many organisations set up with the intention of helping the war effort.

As soon as the conflict began, the people of Frome immediately made
certain of their contribution towards the national war effort that would be
required to support it and ultimately ensure victory. War relief committees
were formed and fund-raising groups established, while everyone from
church-goers to school children either donated or collected everything
from eggs and vegetables to bed-clothing and conkers.

Lady Frances Horner of Mells made an appeal in the local papers
for funds and services for the work a newly formed committee was to
undertake – looking after the wives and families of local soldiers and
sailors now away at war – while the church congregations donated
money through the collecting plate for the Prince of Wales's War Relief
Fund. There were also several appeals in aid of any temporary hospitals
which might be required, especially as news of the mounting casualties
across the English Channel began to filter back home.

Due mainly to the Battle of Ypres, which began in October 1914 and lasted a month, the number of men wounded or killed increased drastically, including many from the Frome area. Among the dead was 17-year-old Private Louis Paynter, of 1/Wiltshires, who had passed for 19 when he enlisted at the beginning of the year, but had, in fact, still been only 16. His mother, who lived at Plumbers Barton in Frome, had tried to persuade him to wait for a couple of years, this being before the war, but to no avail.

Private Louis Paynter, of the Wiltshire Regiment, was only 17 when he died, having enlisted at the age of 16. He has no known grave but his name appears on the Frome War Memorial.

Other local men killed throughout this month included Private Albert Little, also of 1/Wiltshires and who died on the same day as Private Paynter, Corporals Harold Lynch and Charles White (the former having been due to get married the following week), Private Henry Stillman and Private Arthur Charlton. On the last day of October, Privates George Padfield from Frome and Alfred Grace from Mells were killed in action, while Private Arthur Dowling, also from Frome, succumbed to wounds he had previously received. All families would receive the now dreaded official telegram.

If these communications from the War Office contained little more than basic facts surrounding the deaths of their loved ones, then letters from comrades, those who had served and fought alongside them, perhaps offered a little comfort. One such letter was sent to the parents of Corporal Charles White, who died on 21 October. It was written by a fellow corporal in their son's company. It read:

Private Henry Stillman, of the Somerset Light Infantry, had completed nearly nine years service before he died in October 1914. His brother, William, would be killed the following month.

'Dear Sir, No doubt you will wonder who this epistle is from, but I thought it best as an old chum of Charlie's to write and let you know about him, myself. It happened on the 20th at a place near — where we were in the trenches holding the Germans' advance. Charlie with myself and another fellow, were in one hole. The enemy spotted the trenches and we were absolutely a

target for their artillery. You could not lift your head up or else you would have been raked with Maxim gun fire and rifle fire.

A shell burst upon Charlie's head and another's head. A shot went through one fellow and a piece of shell entered Charlie's abdomen, inflicting a big hole there. We had to leave the trenches under heavy fire, but at night time, with the Germans 300 yards away, some fellows got all the wounded to a farmhouse. No medical men being handy all that was possible was done for them.

The men had to leave those there who could not walk, and the next morning we met the farmhouse people coming from their farm owing to the German advance. We asked them how the wounded men were, and through an interpreter we were told that the one shot through the abdomen died during the night. We suffered a lot of casualties during that and the next day. But we were all sorry for "Toosh", as we called Charlie. He was my football chum and he was a great favourite with the men. I am deeply sorry for you all ... '

Another letter, written to the mother of Frome man Arthur Charlton, was again from a fellow comrade of her son, a Private Tipp. In his letter, he said:

'[Arthur] *was killed instantaneously by a machine gun. It occurred about seven o'clock in the morning. We were in the trenches of Ypres, and the enemy started to bombard us. An order to retire was given, and Arthur and I were the last two out of the trenches. We got halfway out, when I got wounded. There was no time to bandage the wound, so Arthur asked me if I could manage to get to a hayrick, about 100 yards away. We got there all right, but we hadn't been there long before we had to get out. Arthur asked if we should go some ten paces from one another in moving away. Arthur was first, and he had not gone far before he was knocked out by a machine gun. I had*

Frome born Arthur Charlton was a private in the Welsh Regiment, when he was killed in October 1914. His parents lived at 11 Redland Terrace, while his marital home was in Bridge Street.

to lay beside the haystack until I was almost scorched on the one
side, but the smoke got so thick that I was able to get away later.
Arthur was missed very much, as he was so happy and used to
cheer the boys up.'

As comforting as these letters might have been, they could not bring
their sons back. Whatever feelings of euphoria had existed in the town
back in August was fading fast with every official telegram delivery, if
it not already completely gone, as the reality of what this war really
meant, in terms of men's lives, was now being felt all around the area.

November 1914 began in the same way October had ended, with
fighting on the Western Front and the deaths of more men. Private John
'Jack' Arthur Avon of 1/Somersets, whose parents lived at Goulds
Ground in Frome, was killed on the first of the month, at Ypres. On the
same day, thousands of miles away in South America, Able Seaman
Reginald Keats was also killed. He died during the Battle of Coronel,
which took place off Cape Coronel in Chile. It was the first major naval
engagement between the two opposing forces' surface vessels (as
opposed to submersibles) and during it, the flagship of the British fleet,
HMS *Good Hope*, a 14,000 ton armoured cruiser, was sunk by the

HMS Good Hope *was the British fleet's flagship but that did not stop it being*
sunk by the enemy on the first day of November 1914. Everyone on board,
including Able Seaman Reginald Keats, was killed.

Germans. Before it met its watery end, there was a huge explosion on board and everyone, including Able Seaman Keats, was killed.

Although the total British casualties reached around 60,000, the Germans failed to break through at Ypres and so this fact, along with their earlier failure to break through at the River Marne, led to a stalemate on the Western Front. Trenches had been dug from the outset of hostilities, but now both sides began construction in earnest and in almost no time at all a continuous network of them stretched from the English Channel to the Swiss border, a distance of nearly 500 miles (800 kilometres). And with this development, it quickly became apparent that any thoughts of this being a short war were now gone.

At the beginning of November a change was made in the amount of time spent on the Western Front. Each company of men would now spend six days in the front line and then three days in what was known as support lines. This change was welcomed by the soldiers, not least

Women were especially employed to undertake the laundering of clothing belonging to soldiers' who were 'out of the lines'.

The soldier in the foreground is trying to get the remaining lice out of his clothing.

because it meant they could have the chance, when out of the lines, to clean themselves and their clothing.

Large buildings, such as breweries or linen factories, were rigged up as washing stations for the men and a routine quickly established. On arriving, the men would take off their service dress (jacket, trousers and cap) and then using their identity tags, would tie them together so they could be taken to the fumigator. The rest of their clothes would be taken off for boiling in disinfectant, while the men, supplied with soap and towels, got into several large makeshift bathtubs, containing hot water. Around ten men would crowd into each one, each bringing with him thousands of lice, so much so that the surface of the bath water would soon become completely covered. Once their bath was complete, the men would receive clean underclothing and have their uniforms returned – piping hot and ironed by women employed for such duties. The whole process for a company, comprising nearly 200

HMS Bulwark. *Having suffered an internal explosion, while anchored in home waters, it sank to the bottom taking with it 800 lives, among them William Stillman and William Wheeler.*

men, would be completed in about an hour and a quarter. It was a welcome break, no doubt, before having to return to the front lines.

Along with Private Avon and Able Seaman Keats, the month of November saw the deaths of Private Frederick Turner, aged 22, of the 1st Battalion South Staffordshire Regiment, Private William Stillman, aged 31, of the Royal Marine Light Infantry and 16-year-old Boy 1st Class William Wheeler. As well as sharing a first name, they were both on HMS *Bulwark* when they were killed. The 15,000 ton battleship was anchored off Sheerness, in the English Channel, when an internal explosion caused it to sink, taking with it nearly 800 men. If news of William Wheeler's death was tragic, especially after he had only recently written to his family to say he had just passed his first class examination and that he was 'still alive and all right', then it was doubly so for William Stillman's

Private William Stillman had served for 12 years in the Royal Marines when he was killed on board HMS Bulwark, *through the internal explosion that sunk the ship. He was 31 years old.*

parents, as he was the second son they had lost in a little over a month. Their younger son, Henry, had been killed in October, while serving with the Somersets.

Since Private Henry Stillman's death, the men of his battalion had spent the whole of November fighting in and around an area known as Ploegsteert Wood, commonly referred to by British soldiers as 'Plugstreet'. With December fast approaching thoughts no doubt began to turn to Christmas and the possible chance of going home on leave. On 10 December, however, all leave was cancelled. The Somersets were to take part in a 'push' that would be made against one of the strongpoints of the German line. This offensive would lead to many more official telegrams being received by families at home.

Meanwhile, for the Wiltshire Regiment, the early part of December saw more fatalities among their ranks: Lance Corporal W. Higgs, aged 22, whose parents lived at Low Water, Frome and Private W. Ashford, aged 23, who lived at Bell Lane, in the town.

Also in December an episode took place that was reported in the *Somerset Standard* early in the New Year. The newspaper had received a letter from a Corporal Bailey detailing a 'chance meeting' that had occurred at a French railway station not long before Christmas. Prior to the war, Corporal William Bailey had been a trainer for Frome Football Club, but by December 1914 was serving as a Military Policeman and found himself in France overseeing the transport of Princess Mary's Christmas gifts for the British troops. While on duty at the wayside station, a train carrying British soldiers pulled in. On calling out 'any Frome boys here', to his surprise the reply came back, 'yes, three of us.' The trio turned out to be Corporals Arthur Long and Willoughby Sweet and Captain Arthur Batten-Pooll. After greeting one another and exchanging small talk about Frome, Corporal Bailey set about organising a meal and before long, the four of them were sitting down to bacon and steak washed down with French coffee. Afterwards they bid their farewells and went their separate ways, with thoughts perhaps of meeting up in Frome once the war had ended.

As the realisation the war would not now be over by Christmas began to sink in though, the festive season arrived in Frome with subdued spirit. With so many men away fighting and the memory of

A typical Christmas card sent from Frome men fighting abroad.

those who had already died for their country painfully fresh, there was an obvious reluctance to celebrate. As the *Somerset Standard* described it:

> *'Christmas is a time for rejoicing, when the heart responds merrily to its gladsome surroundings, but this year the festival has been shorn of its happy associations and joyous festivities and overshadowed with the great national sorrow.'*

Although there were sporadic outpourings of merriment, the message had been heeded as the *Standard* would report in the New Year.

> *'Consequently in Frome as in the rest of the country Christmas was quietly spent, as it should be. Only the callous could have rejoiced with the same merry heart of old, for the knowledge that so many of our fellows were risking their lives on land and sea for the "dear old country" must have subdued the spirits, and the memory of those who have laid down their lives for the cause*

of the fatherland must have had a chastening effect even on the young. As we look back on the festival it is with none of the old memories of happy hours and pleasant gatherings. No one felt in the mood for boisterous rejoicing, but a good effort was made in many homes to be cheerful for the sake of the young. It has indeed been more than ever a festival for the young.'

For any bursts of merriment there were, the perpetrators also had to contend with the weather, which did its best to further dampen already muted spirits. Christmas Eve, for example, was cold and wet and even though Frome streets were crowded and people *'wore cheerful expressions'*, the consensus of opinion was that it was more like a typical Saturday night in the town, rather than the evening before *'the greatest festival of the year'*. Elsewhere, it was reported trains were not as crowded as in previous years, with many of those travelling being soldiers still training in England but home on leave.

From all accounts, it seems shopkeepers were probably among the happiest people in Frome during Christmas, as several experienced record turnovers. For many, the forecast and expectation had been one of gloom and little spending, but this was dispelled with brisk trade and quickly emptying windows. Perhaps understandably, the shops selling toys and sweets were among the busiest and if the reality of war had now begun to sink in with the adults, then the children still wanted to ride the wave of patriotism, with the supply of military toys swiftly becoming exhausted. One mother, as reported in the *Journal*, was overheard trying to soothe her increasingly distraught child, when it became clear the shop had run out of boxes of soldiers, the mother telling her son it was because Lord Kitchener needed all he could get to fight the Germans.

Leading up to Christmas, Frome Post Office, by and large, reported a relatively normal period for both their indoor and outdoor staff, although those working behind the counter reported a large increase of use by the soldiers stationed in the town, or else back on furlough. On Christmas Day itself, the early morning delivery became hampered by abysmal weather conditions. At seven o'clock, as the postmen were setting out on their rounds, the drizzling rain quickly froze, turning

Post Office Staff staff pictured before the war. The year the war started, the Post Office moved from Bath Street to the Market Place.

roads and pavements into sheets of glass. Heavily laden, walking on the slippery pavements could only be accomplished with the greatest of caution, as was the negotiation of steps and other entrances to houses. This ultimately led to rounds taking much longer than normal, but as it was later reported in the paper, '[Postmen] *had the full sympathy of the inhabitants, and nobody grumbled because the first delivery was not as early as usual.'*

The conditions also affected the rest of the town's population, especially those who had gone to the early religious services. The rain, which had been falling on their way to their respective churches, had turned to ice by the time they came out again. This led to numerous falls among the returning congregations, many of them elderly. But it wasn't only those making their way by foot that the weather played havoc with. For those travelling by public transport, journeys were just as bad. Christmas Eve had seen the late arrival of several trains, many of the delays to passenger trains caused by military exigencies, but with the added nuisance of the treacherous ice, delays became increasingly longer. Those travelling to Frome from either Bath or Bristol via Radstock on Christmas morning, for example, had to endure a three-hour journey to finally reach their home station. This was largely due to the train's wheels slipping on the metal tracks. So much so, that for part of the way, up a steep gradient, the stoker had to sprinkle sand on the line to enable the engine and its wheels to gain a grip. A further solution to try and counter this was the division of the train at Paulton and after taking the first two coaches to the next station, the engine returned to collect the rest. The train and its passengers finally reached Frome at one o'clock on Christmas Day afternoon.

Boxing Day, which fell on the Saturday, was as subdued as its predecessor and by the time Monday arrived, it was reported in the *Journal* that time was hanging heavy for many people and that employment, when it resumed, was renewed with more enthusiasm than normal.

When reporting on the demise of Christmas spirit in Frome, the *Standard* had, in all good intention, mused on the fact that perhaps the men in the front lines, with the

The need to stay in contact with friends or family back home was strong and so letters were much sought after and anticipated by Frome men abroad.

A lull in hostilities gives the opportunity to write a letter back home.

image of them singing carols, sharing presents and receiving greetings from home, were perhaps better off and happier than the local population. For many this might have proved true – although no doubt all of them would rather have been at home – but for many others, Christmas gave only a slightest respite, if any at all. Although the Christmas Truce of 1914 has entered the annals of history, with the leaving of trenches, the shaking of hands and gestures of goodwill between opposing soldiers, and even a game of football or two, in reality this 'truce' was confined to only certain sections of the line and only on the Western Front. Elsewhere, for example, Ernie Brooks, a driver with the Royal Field Artillery, who before the war had worked for Mr E.J. Hoddinott, of Witham Hall Farm, Frome, wrote to his former employer to tell him that: *'This is Christmas Day, and there are plenty of shells for presents to start with.'* At the same time, several soldiers died on that day or ones surrounding it, usually succumbing to wounds acquired earlier in the month.

For certain Frome families, however, the festive period did reunite them with loved ones, however fleeting. Able Seaman Bert Burr, serving with HMS *Cumberland* spent a 'short holiday', as reported in

Many of the cards sent to their loved ones by soldiers overseas were embroidered.

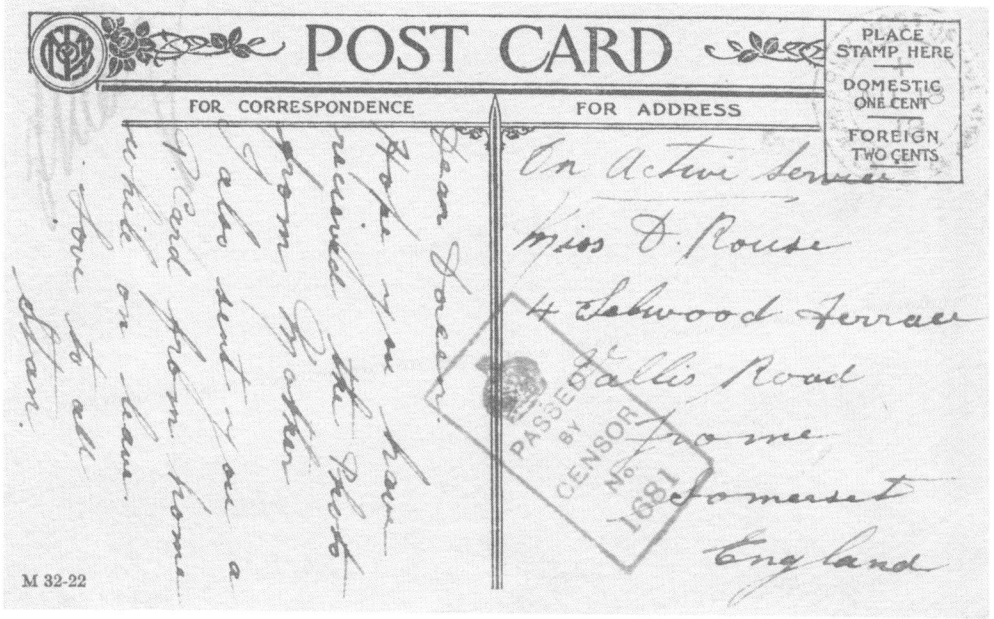

A postcard that has been sent 'back home' to Frome and which has been passed by the censor.

the *Standard*, with his parents in Frome. Having left England in August, he had been away for five months in the Cameroons, where he had caught malaria.

Another reunion took place in the early hours of New Year's Day. Having walked from Trowbridge, Trooper W. Parfitt, of the Royal Horse Guards, arrived at his home in Keyford Place in Frome around four o'clock in the morning. It was really a flying visit – only having a seventy-two hour furlough – to see his wife and children, but by all accounts was worth the effort. Even though Trooper Parfitt had been at the front since October, his wife was reported as saying: *'I had never seen him looking so well during all the twelve years we have been married'*.

Where 'truces' were in place on the Western Front, it also gave both sides the opportunity to recover their dead from no man's land – the area existing between opposing trenches – and give them a decent burial. One of the men recovered and buried on Christmas Day was 18-year-old Private Herbert 'Bert' Frank Miller, of 1/Somersets, whose parents lived at 149 The Butts, Frome. On the outbreak of war he had enlisted and was sent to Devonport to undertake training in the regiment's 3rd (Special Reserve) Battalion. On completion, he was sent to France. His body was recovered from no man's land with twenty others from his regiment. Many, if not all, of the men had been killed while attacking the 'Birdcage', a strongly defended German position – the quantity of wire surrounding it giving rise to its nickname – in the part of Ploegsteert Wood earmarked for the December 'push' that had seen all leave cancelled. The attack took place on 19 December, but the men had to advance over almost impassable ground and several were killed by enemy machine guns. Although managing to occupy a few buildings within the German position and engaging in bitter hand to hand combat, the 1/Somersets' position was soon realised to be untenable and they were forced to withdraw.

In total, five officers of the 1/Somersets and twenty-seven men, including 'Bert' Miller were killed, with another fifty-two wounded and thirty more missing. It was yet another loss of life which followed on from those of the previous few months. In fact, since they had left England, towards the end of August, the 1/Somersets had lost 36 of their officers and more than 1,150 from the other ranks, including many of the reinforcements who had subsequently come across. And out of the original 1,000 men who had made the journey back then, only 270 men remained.

Private Herbert Miller. Like some others from Frome, Bert was 18 when he died.

It would not be until the New Year that the Millers would learn of their son's death, but there were inklings of it in a letter sent to them by his brother, Henry, also with 1/Somersets,.

'We have been in the trenches for about two weeks. We had to face an attack last Saturday, and I can tell you we had a hot time of it for about four hours. We lost all our officers and about 100 men out of 170. I was laying in one place for about two hours. Bert was in the same charge, and I don't know how he got on. F. Crook is in the same company, and he said he had not seen him since. I hope he was not killed. When he (Crook) told me I could *have dropped. He may be wounded and taken back to hospital. We are having a rest from the 22nd to the 27th December. We received Princess Mary's gift to-day* [every soldier received one and it included tobacco, cigarettes and a pipe] *and it was a very nice one. We have had a poor Christmas, but we must make up for it when we come home.'*

After his brother's fate was known, Henry would write to their parents again to say that

'I am sorry to tell you, that Bert was killed, and was buried on Christmas Day, by H. Newport [a fellow Fromite] *and W. May with 17 others. I understand that they had to walk into certain death. Those against us were three times our number, and I am lucky to be alive myself.'*

As it turned out, those final words would turn out to be prophetic.

For the majority of sections on the front line, where a 'truce' was in place, this lasted until the end of the month and allowed an extended respite for the exhausted troops. Back in Frome, however, the year's end brought for many more misery and heartache. The end of December 1914 in Frome brought with it snowstorms and torrential rain, the result being extensive flooding of large areas of the town. The *Somerset & Wilts Journal* reported one Frome resident as saying:

'Not for eleven years has the water been so high and so much inconvenience experienced in this part of town as was the case on Monday night, when some of us were about until 4 o'clock the next morning taking measures to prevent the flooding of our houses or helping those who had slept peacefully while the water rose nine or ten inches deep in their downstairs rooms, causing considerable work and some damage to carpets, and sundry articles of furniture.'

This resident lived at Willow Vale which runs parallel to the River Frome, and although at the start of the century it had not been an unusual experience for that area, and the nearby Market Place, to be

Willow Vale under water after the River Frome bursts its banks.

The Market Place completely flooded.

flooded after continuous heavy rain, much flood prevention work had been undertaken in the intervening years. For example, several obstructions had been removed from the bed of the river, and in places the bed had actually been lowered, along with more careful attention to the hatches below the Town Bridge. With a heavy rainfall throughout December resulting in the land adjoining the river becoming water-logged, and another heavy fall of rain on the Monday after Christmas, which itself was followed by a blinding snowstorm, this all culminated in the River Frome bursting its banks.

At Willow Vale this happened about ten o'clock in the evening, late enough for many residents to have already gone to bed thinking nothing was amiss. Those with past experience of the floods, however, stayed awake and busied themselves in rearranging furniture and carpets in anticipation. Boards were then nailed over any potential openings and 'hatches' placed in front of doors, securing them with clay to make them watertight. Around midnight the water had risen to around eighteen inches in front of the lower houses in Willow Vale, and began to seep into those buildings unprepared, coming through the floor boards and ruining carpets and furniture; and then, after receding, leaving a nasty smelling sediment to be cleaned up.

As the floods expanded ever outward, more areas of the town centre became affected. Water came pouring into Market Place, it was later reported, *'from the passage at the side of Messrs. Newport and Son's shop and from the Blue Boar Inn, it quickly covered a good part of the roadway.'* The inn yard had so much water that around midnight several horses stabled there had to be rescued by soldiers. The water reached its highest level between two and three o'clock in the morning, then slowly began to recede, leaving behind considerable damage to be attended to in the New Year.

However unwelcome the flooding was, it nevertheless provided a temporary distraction from a war that had overshadowed all aspects of everyday life during the last few months. But if the events of 1914 had plunged Frome and the rest of the country into a world almost unimaginable back in the summer, then it was only a taste of things to come in the following weeks, months and years.

CHAPTER 3

Deepening Conflict (Jan–Jun 1915)

'Today we enter another year, another milestone in the journey of life has been reached, a fresh chapter in our national and individual history has been commenced, and although "hope springs eternal in the human breast", we enter 1915 with fearsome misgivings as to the future, which lies dark and unknown before us.'

These words were published in the New Year's Day edition of the *Somerset & Wilts Journal* and although the future was 'dark and unknown', the paper was defiant in its opinion that at least the previous year was now over. *'As the old year lay a dying last evening and the bell tolled its requiem,'* the editorial proclaimed, *'it was with a sense of relief that the public adopted the words of Tennyson, "The year is going, let him go", for it can be truly said that 1914 brought us more evil than good and has taken more than it has given.'*

At the start of 1915 the reality that this was not going to be a short war had become abundantly clear. The conflict was spreading to almost every part of the globe and in doing so, brought in nations such as Italy, Bulgaria and Turkey, as well as numerous colonies of the imperial powers; in Britain's case, these included Dominions such as Australia, New Zealand, Canada and India.

For many Frome families the New Year was anything but happy.

If the fighting spirit was still there, both at home and abroad, along with the belief that 'right' would finally triumph, then exactly when this would happen was much less certain. As the *Journal* put it:

> *'Although we enter the unknown year with all the old faith that right must triumph, there is less confidence as to what the future may have in store for us. All that we know for certain is that we are in the throes of a deadly and terrible war, and no one… can foretell when the last blow will be struck and the last shot fired. Still we have faith in our causes, and believe that our arms and those of our Allies will be victorious, but we know not what sacrifice we shall have to make and what hardship and suffering we shall be called upon to endure before the Kaiser's forces are vanquished and the peace of Europe is once more restored on a firm and permanent basis.'*

For numerous families in Frome and the surrounding villages the 'sacrifice' they would have to make and the 'hardship and suffering' they would have to endure, revolved around the loss of loved ones. Too many had already received a fateful telegram, but for several

THE CONSOLER.

HAROLD COPPING, PINX.

I will not leave you comfortless

St John XIV 18

The Consoler: a postcard showing a far too familiar scene of bereavement.

households the opening months of the war had already delivered a double tragedy. One family was the Stillmans, who lived at 2, The Retreat, Frome. As mentioned previously, they had lost one son, William, in November and another, Henry, the preceding month. Henry had been serving with 1/Somersets and his parents had only received a letter from him the week before he was killed. In it, he recounted how he had been through the Battle of Mons, during which a piece of shell had passed through the sleeve of his coat but had left him unharmed.

Another set of parents to experience the death of two sons by early 1915 were the Millers of 149, The Butts, Frome. Although Private Bert Miller had been killed before Christmas, his mother and father did not receive the news until into the New Year. Before January was out, they would be informed that their eldest son had also been killed. Private Henry Charles Miller had served in the local Territorials before the war and had joined the National Reserve. At the time he was called up he was working at the Selwood Printing Works of Butler & Tanner in Frome. In the *Somerset & Wilts Journal* dated Friday, 4 September 1914, his name appeared as having been accepted into Lord Kitchener's new force [along with that of Herbert Newport, of 44 Broadway, Frome – see below]. Like his brother, Henry underwent training before being sent to the Western Front to join 1/Somersets.

Herbert Newport was one of the men who had buried Bert on Christmas Day – as part of his duties as a company stretcher bearer – and he now wrote a letter to the brothers' parents about the circumstances surrounding the death of Henry, or 'Harry' as his comrades called him.

> *'Harry was wounded in the stomach this morning. I was one of the stretcher-bearers who brought him in. The doctor attended him, then we took him to our dressing station and from there he was moved to hospital. Harry was quite conscious and bearing up well and asked me if I would write to you. My sympathy is with you at this added trouble. May God give you strength to bear it. He promises us "As thy burden, so shall thy strength be", with kind regards... Herbert H. Newport (one of Harry's comrades).'*

A second letter was received by the Millers, this time from one of the sisters on duty at the casualty clearing station:

> *'I am sorry to inform you of the death of your son, 7330, Private*

Miller, Somerset Light Infantry. He was brought in here yesterday, January 18th, very severely wounded, everything possible has been done for his comfort by the surgeons and nurses, but there was no hope for his recovery and he died soon after he was admitted. He was conscious until shortly before he passed away and he asked me to write and tell you that he had been wounded and to give you his love. He was feeling too ill to talk much. He was visited by the chaplain. Your son will be buried in the churchyard here. I am sorry I cannot tell you the name of the place, but it is against the army regulations to do so. All your son's personal belongings will be forwarded through headquarters, believe me, yours truly, K. Mathews (sister).'

In fact, Private Henry Miller was buried at Bailleul Communal Cemetery, in Nord, France, while the final resting place of his brother, Bert, was the Ploegsteert Wood Military Cemetery in Belgium.

Among the great changes the First World War brought into being was the way in which those who died serving their country were commemorated. Up until the beginning of the twentieth century, those who died on the battlefield would more often than not be buried in communal graves near the site, with little, if any, markings to designate their location. Paradoxically, the sheer number of deaths in this conflict necessitated a distinct change in attitude and an effort to mark individual deaths came into being. This ultimately led in 1917 to the creation of the Imperial War Graves Commission (from 1960 the Commonwealth War Graves Commission – CWGC), which would organise, build and maintain cemeteries around the world commemorating those soldiers from British, Imperial and later Commonwealth forces who died during the First World War (and then, the Second World War as well). In the present day, the Commission oversees these memorials in more than 150 countries worldwide.

An individual grave could only be created, however, if there were enough remains of a body to be buried. The nature of the First World War meant hundreds of thousands of men were literally 'blown to bits', either by artillery shells or other explosive devices, or else were

Women tending to the graves of fallen British soldiers.

deemed 'missing in action'. This could be through a multitude of
causes, although one of the most horrendous must surely be the fate
that befell so many soldiers on the Western Front – that of literally
being sucked under the treacherous quagmires of mud created through
the fighting, with no chance of recovering the body.

In these cases, plaques or rolls of honour would be created in
designated places, with the names of the dead added to memorials
deemed closest to the spot where they were last known to have been.
The only problem with the location of these memorials and graves
which existed, was that they could be anywhere in the world and so
the majority of grieving relatives were unable to visit them. To counter
this, many tens of thousands of photographs of graves or rolls of honour
were sent out on request to families, while at the same time memorials
of one kind or another were erected in towns and cities across Britain,
including Frome.

In the decades that followed, of course, foreign travel would become more and more accessible to the majority of people, so much so that many of those who had lost loved ones, or else their descendants, could finally make the pilgrimage to pay their respects. One such example was reported in the *Frome Times* dated 14 August 2014. Debbie Christmas, whose great-great-uncles had been the Stillman brothers, wrote to the newspaper to say she had recently visited the Ploegsteert Memorial to the Missing in Belgium, where Henry Stillman was commemorated. His brother, William, was commemorated on the Portsmouth Naval Memorial. Both also appear on the memorial roll of honour in Frome's Memorial Theatre.

A section of the Frome War memorial, listing men who died during the First World War.

Egypt was just one of many countries where men from Frome found themselves stationed.

Men from the Frome area served and were killed in many parts of the world and one way they could find themselves there was if they had joined the Royal Navy, but it wasn't just through the navy they found themselves deployed to foreign, often exotic, locations. And as dangerous as it might be engaging the enemy once there, for many local men who survived the war, the chance to have travelled abroad would be an experience of a lifetime, one they would never have had if they had just stayed in Frome working for one of the local factories or businesses. Some of the countries these men visited, while serving with their regiments or ships, included Turkey, Cameroon, Africa, Egypt, Greece, Mesopotamia, Palestine and India.

With these unfamiliar locations, however, came another threat: disease. Even when fighting had temporarily ceased, Frome men were still dying from illness and disease. Men like Private Herbert Baker of the 9th Battalion King's Own (Royal Lancaster Regiment) who died of fever in Salonika, Private Reginald Stockting of the 256th Company, Machine Gun Corps, who caught malaria and died in India and Colour Sergeant Ernest Barnes of the Army Service Corps, who recovered from a severe attack of fever while in South Africa, only to die not long after from pneumonia.

Frederick George in Egypt 1915.

When fighting did resume, however, the number of fatalities it caused dwarfed any nature could muster (or until 1918, at least). In the spring of 1915 plans which had been drawn up during the previous winter months were put into action. With Turkey now in the war, an offensive was devised by Winston Churchill – at the time First Lord of

British Troops in Mesopotamia escort captured Turkish prisoners through the streets of Baghdad.

the Admiralty – to undermine this new German ally. The campaign though, ultimately became one of the worst disasters of the war, with Churchill being forced to resign his position over it. Of all the land battles and campaigns in the theatres of war that took place outside of the Western Front, throughout the First World War, perhaps only this one – Gallipoli – can be compared with the 'disasters' such as Ypres, the Somme, Verdun or Passchendaele.

Once Turkey entered the war on Germany's side, it meant Britain's interests in Persia, along with its dependence on the Suez Canal, were threatened. At the same time as safeguarding the supply lines to India and the East, it was agreed a diversionary attack elsewhere might be a way to break the deadlock on the Western Front. After a disastrous naval attack, in which the Allies lost six battleships, a naval bombardment

Frome-born Private Herbert Baker of the Royal Lancaster Regiment. He died in Salonika of fever, in the last year of the war, leaving a widow and three young children back in England.

followed by the landing of ground troops was put into action. As the number of men required for such a campaign could not be taken from the Western Front, a force of 70,000 men from the Australian and New Zealand Army Corps (ANZACS) was deployed. The campaign's objective was to land men on the Gallipoli Peninsula, in the Dardanelles, and then move northwards to capture Constantinople. Disaster occurred from the very outset: the Turks had realised what was happening and so were well-prepared to repel the attack; the Australians landed at the wrong cove; and in places the depth of the water had been totally underestimated, leaving the soldiers, unable to wade ashore, as sitting targets and so swiftly turning the sea into one awash with crimson.

It is perhaps natural to wonder how men from the Frome area might have been involved in this campaign, but involved they were. Many had emigrated before the war and then enlisted in the ANZACS at the outbreak of it. One such man was Private Henry Crees. He left England in 1909, his parents remaining in Frome, although he had been living in Bruton immediately prior to going. He was serving with the 13th Battalion Australian Infantry Force when he was killed nine days into the campaign.

Private Henry Crees was killed during the ill-fated Gallipoli campaign. He has no known grave but his name appears on the Frome War Memorial.

There were British units present as well though, and included the 1st Battalion Essex Regiment. Serving with them was 18-year-old Private Thomas Edwards, formerly of the Royal Artillery, whose parents lived at Bowns Cottage, Critchill, Frome. He was seriously wounded and later died from his wounds. He was buried at Hill 10 Cemetery in Turkey. Others included Private Richard Franklin and Sergeant Phillip Alder, both from Frome and serving with the 4th Battalion South Wales Borderers, and Sergeant William Couch of the 5th Battalion Royal Irish Regiment, who came from Rode. All three men died during August 1915.

Like those on the Western Front earlier, the Gallipoli campaign eventually became another stalemate with opposing trenches, in places, only hundreds of feet apart. Disease then began to cause more deaths than bullets, especially at the height of the blistering summer and the already awful conditions became intolerable. In the end, after several months of fighting, the campaign was ended and the troops withdrawn. Despite the best efforts of the War Office and associated departments, no amount of subterfuge or propaganda could cover the fact this was one of the most humiliating and disastrous episodes in this conflict.

Sergeant William Couch. Like Henry Crees, he was killed in action at Gallipoli and has no known grave. He is commemorated on the Helles Memorial, however, along with 20,000 men.

Another 'disastrous' episode occurred in spring 1915, but this time it was closer to home and no lives were lost. According to the report in the *Somerset Standard* dated 7 May 1915:

> *'A squadron* [of North Somerset Yeomanry] *was sent to defend Frome against a mock attack by the rest of the regiment. Unfortunately, the defending soldiers chose the wrong point at which to base their defence and the rest of the regiment simply marched straight into the town. In fact they may be said to have been in possession of the town before the defenders were aware of their presence. Not a shot was fired, even in pretence.'*

Gallipoli aside, in war the use of propaganda – defined as 'a plan to spread opinions and principles especially to effect change and influence behaviour' – can be a powerful weapon in the struggle for victory. The First World War proved to be no different and all sides involved in the conflict used every means available to influence, mislead or outrage their own people, while at the same time trying to demoralise those of the enemy.

By the end of August 1914, for example, numerous stories of German atrocities in Belgium were circulating freely – courtesy mostly of the press – within England. Tales of nuns being raped, corpses of British soldiers being boiled to use their body fat as grease or tallow and babies being cold-bloodedly bayoneted, were among the most lurid

For many Belgian refugees they would find a safe haven in Frome.

examples. These were, for the most part, creations of government officials or newspaper reporters, but the people of Frome were able to learn the truth for themselves, from the lips of the very people who had lived through it.

As news reached Frome of the million or so Belgians who had been made homeless, either voluntarily or forced, due to the advancing German Army, the Frome Refugee Committee was quickly organised and a decision made to take fifty refugees. By mid-September 1914, nearly half had arrived in the town and by the month's end, all of them had been welcomed on arrival at Frome railway station by the hastily arranged reception committee. This 'welcome' included cake and confectionary, courtesy of Mr W. Bloodsworth, head of the committee and owner of a shop opposite the station.

The majority of these refugees were women and children from Antwerp and Ostend, whose stories were told through a swiftly summoned translator who could speak Flemish. Although bayoneting babies and boiling dead soldiers may have been the realm of journalistic imagination, the reality of what occurred was almost as horrific, barbaric and terrifying. The *Journal* reported, in the words of the refugees themselves and *'without embellishment'*, tales of burnt and looted homes, friends and relatives shot in cold blood, and other acts and outrages *'committed upon women and children under the eyes of husbands and brothers and fathers powerless to protect them'* which the newspaper deemed unfit to print.

One story of German savagery the *Journal* did publish, however, related to the town of Aerschot, where several of the refugees, now safe in Frome, had lived comfortably before the war. When the Germans descended on the town the heavily outnumbered company of Belgian infantrymen had withdrawn to Louvain, a few miles away. The first couple of days had been uneventful but then the German cavalry had arrived and with them *'horror upon horror was loosed upon the inhabitants.'* On the pretence of being fired upon by the local population, front doors had been battered in with rifles and indiscriminate shooting in the streets began. Five hundred men and boys were rounded up and marched, with hands raised, to a nearby field to be shot, or so they were told. As it transpired, most were freed in the evening. There were many killings though and most were in cold blood, two of the victims being the town Burgomaster and his son. Others who were shot had been told they were now free and ordered to run away as quickly as possible, only to be 'picked off' after twenty yards or so by laughing German 'marksmen'. The *Journal* continued:

> *'Meantime, the women and children were herded in the streets, the women being forced to kneel with hands raised above their heads. In that position they watched the burning of their homes. One old lady of 99, four years bedridden, was dragged on her bed into the street, while her house was given to the flames before her eyes.'*

A few days later the Germans moved on – leaving around 150 civilians dead – but hearing more cavalry were on their way, the remaining townspeople fled, eventually ending up in England, with many finding sanctuary in the welcoming arms of Frome and its people.

Even without the Belgian refugees' testimonies and the paranoia surrounding the spy 'threat', being a German in Frome was, to say the least, uncomfortable. Matters were made worse by the restrictions imposed at the outbreak of war by the introduction of the Aliens

The arrival of German cavalry forced many Belgians to flee their homes.

Restriction Act. This obliged all foreign residents in Frome, as elsewhere, to register with the local police station, giving their full name, address, status and employment. After their photograph was taken, they were then informed that their movements were restricted to a five-mile radius from the town, outside which they would require permission. Locals were actively encouraged to inform the police of the names of any German subjects living in the neighbourhood, while advertisers used patriotic sentiment to sell products. Prossers of 20, Market Place, Frome for instance, proclaimed in a newspaper advert that *'The Public will be performing a Patriotic Action by assisting English Manufacturers to keep business moving, and their men employed, by buying ENGLISH PIANOS ONLY.'* At the same time, organisations such as the Royal Automobile Club (RAC) banned members of German or Austrian origin, property and possessions of wealthy Germans were seized and it was even considered unpatriotic to own a dachshund dog!

One German, who had married a local servant, Ellen Daniell, did not stay around long enough to experience any hostility, immediately

A patriotic advertisement.

deserting his wife and fleeing back to his home country, leaving her in Frome with the surname of Schult, a recently born son called Otto and desperately alone. Many Germans who stayed in England, through choice or circumstances, changed their surnames to more 'acceptable' ones and several even tried to join the British Army to prove where their loyalty lay. (Even the British Royal family changed their name during the war, from the Germanic Saxe-Coburg-Gotha to Windsor.)

If the anti-German feeling that existed during the opening few months of the war had mellowed by early 1915, it was soon enflamed once more by an incident that was 'manna from heaven' for the British propaganda machine. Apart from very brief periods of time, German U-boats operated under restricted action. This meant, for example, they would surface and allow crews of merchant ships to take to the lifeboats and escape before sinking their vessels. By the time the British liner *Lusitania* sailed from New York, bound for Liverpool, the U-boats were operating on orders of unrestricted action, meaning the seas around Britain were declared a war zone and any ship entering them could expect to be sunk without warning. This is exactly what happened to the *Lusitania*, off the coast of southern Ireland, on 7 May 1915. It took around twenty minutes for the transatlantic liner to sink, after being torpedoed, taking with her around 1,100 passengers and crew. The resultant worldwide outrage and condemnation did not seem to phaze the Germans – their own press having reported it as an 'outstanding success' – but one of the consequences of this action was that it ultimately brought the United States into the war, there having been more than 120 Americans who died in the attack.

The early months of 1915 had been relatively quiet in the trenches, due to the very cold winter, with little happening in terms of offensive movements on either side. At the first signs of spring, preparations began to put into action the plans decided upon during the 'lull' in the war and which, it was hoped, would break the stalemate. These plans had included the Gallipoli Campaign, but on the Western Front, the opening salvo was an attack on the village of Neuve Chapelle, in north-eastern France. After a short, but intense, bombardment by the British artillery – the heaviest up to that point in the war – the infantry pressed forward. Although progress was made initially, with the village falling into British hands, two major issues were highlighted which would have far reaching effects later in the war.

The first was the shortage of shells on the British side. The Shell Crisis, as it became known, contributed to a change of government but would eventually be addressed through an increase in production back in Britain. The second issue facing the British was the cost in human lives to secure victory, which mainly came about through the tactics currently employed. At Neuve Chapelle solid walls of men walked side-by-side and were slaughtered by German machine guns, behind their strongly defended positions. And, as if to add horror to tragedy, as soon as one line was annihilated, another moved forward to take its place, with the same outcome. If the soldiers were only obeying orders, then the real evil came not from the German machine gunners who mowed line after line of them down, but from the General Staff – safe in their HQs far behind the frontline – who followed this pattern of attack continuously in the months to come.

Private William Cottrell of the Worcestershire Regiment. He was killed in action on 13 March 1915, aged 30. He has no known grave.

The Battle of Neuve Chapelle lasted four days and amongst those killed from the Frome area were 30-year-old Private William Cottrell of the 1/Worcestershires, whose parents previously lived at Rode and 34-year-old Private Frederick Nicholas of 2/Wiltshires, who had been born in Beckington. He was reported as 'missing in action' and it was only a year or so later, when he could not be traced as a prisoner of war, the War Office *'had been regretfully constrained to conclude that he was dead, and that his death took place on the 12th of March 1915.'* Neither soldier has a known grave, both being commemorated on the Le Touret Memorial in France.

The following month, April, saw fighting on more 'familiar' territory: that of Ypres. It was here during the previous October and November several Frome men had lost their lives: including Arthur Charlton, Louis Paynter and Henry Stillman. This Second Battle of Ypres, although in many ways similar to the first, has become infamous in the annals of warfare due to the fact it was during this battle the Germans used a new weapon they had developed: gas. Chemical warfare had arrived.

The unwitting soldiers first to feel the effect of chlorine gas were French colonial troops – who fled in panic – followed two days later by the Canadians. The Canadians stood their ground, however, and tied urine-soaked cloths over their mouths and nostrils, as it was known ammonia present in urine decreased the effects of the gas. British soldiers though, including men from Frome, would encounter this terrible weapon only too soon.

If the Germans were branded 'evil' and cowardly for the 'atrocities' they had committed, then British soldiers were elevated to the position of heroic. Although most of the men fighting on the front line carried out their duties commendably, on many occasions certain acts of bravery went above this call of duty and were rewarded by honours. Many men from Frome and its surrounding villages were to receive such recognition throughout the war.

Private Edgar Bush, recipient of the Distinguished Conduct Medal.

As early as August 1914, the opening month of the war, Private Edgar Bush, serving with the 3rd (King's Own) Hussars became the first Frome man to be decorated. In recognition of his actions during the British withdrawal after the Battle of Mons, he was awarded a Distinguished Conduct Medal (DCM), the highest award for gallantry after the Victoria Cross. Edgar was the son of Mr and Mrs Timothy Bush who lived in Willow Vale, the area of town running alongside the River Frome and which had experienced some of the worst of the flooding at the end of December 1914. He had joined the service seven years previously and when war broke out the regiment was stationed at Shorncliffe in Kent. The 3/Hussars, a cavalry unit, went to France on 17 August 1914, as part of the British Expeditionary Force, and took part in the Battle of Mons. It was after this battle that Private Bush performed his act of heroism for which he was decorated. The citation read:

> '3835 Private E. Bush, 3rd Hussars. For the gallantry and coolness displayed at Longeuil on 30th August 1914, when on patrol duty he successfully ambushed ten German cavalrymen.'

Private Bush, along with a comrade, had become parted from their company, when they saw a nearby German patrol. They hid in a straw stack as the patrol passed by and then warned the rest of the company. All of the Germans were killed in the ensuing fire fight.

The Distinguished Conduct Medal which Private Bush was awarded had been established in 1854, during the Crimean War, by Queen

Victoria, and was given for 'distinguished, gallant and good conduct in the field' for non-commissioned officers. It was the 'other ranks' equivalent to the Distinguished Service Order (DSO), awarded to commissioned officers.

In May 1915, after receiving a notification that he was to be awarded the medal, Edgar wrote to his parents at Willow Vale to tell them the news. *'You will be pleased to hear I have been awarded the DCM... I think it is a big honour, don't you?'*

On the same day his parents received his letter he sat down and wrote another to his brother. *'I don't think I told you, did I that I have got the DCM? I was rather surprised when I heard of it, but the captain told me if anyone deserved it I did. So I guess I earned it somewhere.'* Also in this second letter is a reference to the deadly new weapon introduced at Ypres.

> *'We thought we were going to catch it on Sunday when the Germans started using gas, but it did not quite reach us, and our infantry did not half pay them when they started to come out. However, we scraped through once more.'*

Seven months after Private Bush's bravery another soldier, who would later have a Frome connection, showed extreme bravery in the heat of battle and for this action was recognised by the ultimate military decoration: The Victoria Cross.

The Victoria Cross (VC) is the most prestigious medal that can be awarded in the British and Commonwealth Forces and its recipients are given it for the 'most conspicuous bravery, or some daring or pre-eminent act of valour or self-sacrifice, or extreme devotion to duty in the presence of the enemy'. The VC was established two years after the DCM, again by Queen Victoria.

The man to receive this medal was Lance Corporal Wilfred Dolby Fuller, who after the war moved to Frome, where he spent the remainder of his life. He is buried in the town, in Christchurch graveyard. Lance Corporal Fuller was a member of the Grenadier Guards and the action for which his bravery was recognised took place during the Battle of Neuve Chapelle in March 1915. This was the action in which Privates Cottrell and Nicholas were killed. The announcement of his award, along with that of several other recipients, was reported in the second supplement to *The London Gazette* dated Friday, 16 April 1915.

> *'His Majesty the KING has been graciously pleased to approve of the grant of the Victoria Cross to the undermentioned Officer, Non-commissioned Officer and Men for their conspicuous acts of bravery and devotion to duty whilst serving with the Expeditionary Force:- No. 15624 Lance-Corporal Wilfred Dolby Fuller, 1st Battalion, Grenadier Guards. For most conspicuous bravery at Neuve Chapelle on 12th March, 1915. Seeing a party of the enemy endeavouring to escape along a communication trench, he ran towards them and killed the leading man with a bomb; the remainder (nearly 50) finding no means of evading his bombs, surrendered to him. Lance-Corporal Fuller was quite alone at the time.'*

Several of the VCs awarded during this encounter were to soldiers who had used 'bombs', crudely made, hand-thrown charges with short lengths of fuses attached to them. These were normally lit with a cigarette and empty jam jars were popular for the bomb 'casing'.

Throughout the remainder of the war men from Frome and the surrounding area would continue to distinguish themselves in action and be decorated accordingly. This included another recipient of the Victoria Cross: Lieutenant Arthur Batten-Pooll of the 3rd Battalion, Royal Munster Fusiliers, from Rode; he was one of the quartet involved in the 'chance meeting' incident in December 1914, although the circumstances surrounding his act of bravery will be told later.

It was not only men that responded bravely under fire and in the heat of battle, but also animals and, in many ways, these are the unsung heroes of the entire war. Their story and contribution to the war effort will be told in the following chapter.

CHAPTER 4

And the Fight Goes On (Jul–Dec 1915)

During the First World War it wasn't only men (and women) who served in the different theatres of conflict, a whole array of animals were also 'enlisted' to help support the war effort. These included everything from mules, donkeys and oxen to pigeons, dogs and even camels. Probably the most iconic animal that took part in the war though – and the one most associated with it – was the horse.

It wasn't just men who were vulnerable to the horrible new weapon of war introduced by the Germans at Ypres.

It is estimated that more than one million horses were sent for use by the British Army between 1914 and 1918, mainly on the Western Front, and of those one million, only about 60,000 returned. It wasn't just the huge loss of life which was so terrible, but also the fact that along with the demise of their horses, a whole way of life for vast sections of the population was gone forever. The fundamental shift in the rural (and to a lesser degree urban) landscape was felt no more so than in places like Frome, with its thriving industries and businesses dependent on horses within the town's boundaries, and farmers living off the land in the outlying countryside. Although this was a process which had already begun with the industrial revolution, the First World War dealt it an almighty final blow.

When it became certain war was imminent it was calculated that in addition to the horses already attached to specific army regiments, such as the cavalry and artillery, along with infantry ones and other support units, another 25,000 horses were needed immediately. War Office agents were sent out across the country in order to requisition those

It was not only Germans that horses and those who used them had to contend with on the Western Front.

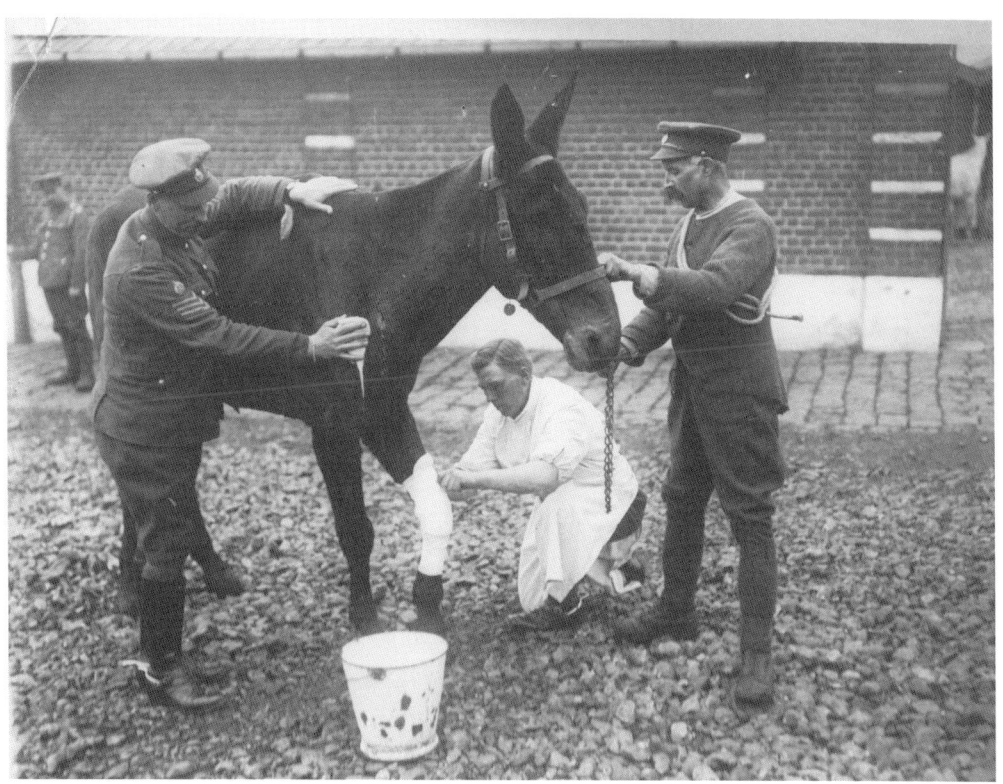

In many ways the horse was the life blood of the army and so had to be looked after well.

horses that were available and whose owners had fortuitously registered them before the war.

While the Army Act of 1881 had given the military the right to seize horses (and carriages) in an emergency – within strict terms laid down by the Act though – the Remount Department, created six years later, was given the responsibility of providing the horses in such a situation. The Act required local authorities to maintain 'a list of persons liable to furnish carriages and animals'. The Remount Department also developed its own registration scheme, whereby 'owners of horses could register a proportion of their horses under an agreement to produce a number of horses at a fixed price in the event of their being required.'

By 1914 the Remount Department had become part of the Army Service Corps, responsible for the provision and training of horses and

Many businesses suddenly found themselves without means of transport.

mules for all other army units. It was a relatively small organisation within the British Army – although it would be expanded as the war continued – but had a large responsibility and a huge undertaking ahead of it. Agents working on behalf of the Remount Service criss-crossed the country to requisition horses registered by their owners, while at the same time, the agents were looking for any other horses they could find that were 'fit for active service'. The majority of the horses required were draft (or dray) horses – from the Old English word 'dragan' which meant 'to draw or haul' – as opposed to horses suitable as cavalry mounts.

As related earlier, War Office agents arrived in Frome on the Wednesday after war had been declared on Germany. This was market day in the town and at once they began requisitioning horses, whether they were on the register or not. Some owners were less willing to part with their animals than others – as no doubt thoughts of harvest time were on their mind – but as most people in Frome believed the war would be ended by Christmas, so the majority of horse owners patriotically handed over their animals amicably enough. Each man would then be given the regulation £40 per horse, once it had passed its medical examination. For this, the animals were rounded up and taken to the exterior of the police station, in Christchurch Street West, where they were examined by veterinary surgeons, brought in especially for the task. They were then walked along the street several times to check their fitness.

The *Somerset & Wilts Journal* reported *'remarkable scenes'* at the market with the wholesale commandeering of suitable horses by Army authorities, while the *Somerset Standard* reported the sight outside the police station, with all the activity going on, to be *'like a fair'*. In truth, out of the fifty-six horses required from the district only twenty-three were selected, as the rest failed the examination. The outstanding horses were obtained the following day from various places in and around the area. The Lamb Brewery Company was compelled to sell several of its horses, while more were requisitioned from the nearby hostelries, used by locals for stabling purposes. Carters were stopped on their rounds, as was anyone in possession of an animal deemed possibly fit for Army service.

Once the required number of horses was obtained, they were then sent to their respective Army units via the Remount Department. The vast majority were put to work as transport animals, trained alongside mules and donkeys to pull anything from gun carriages and heavy field artillery to ambulances and supply wagons. From this it can be seen that although in certain sections of the armed forces the role of horses had diminished, to the point of being obsolete, in the transporting of men, munitions and supplies it had become indispensable.

One example of this 'diminishment' was the cavalry, which had changed almost irreversibly at the onset of the First World War. With development of mechanised weapons, such as rapid firing machine guns and heavy artillery (along with the appearance of the tank and aeroplane later in the conflict) the effectiveness of mounted regiments was severely reduced and so many became 'dismounted' units; the cavalrymen for all intents and purpose becoming foot soldiers. The traditional use of mounted units in the army did still play a part, but this was in hostile terrain, such as in India, Palestine and Mesopotamia, which was more suited to that kind of warfare.

One local firm, Selwood Wagon Works, had three horses requisitioned and perhaps their story can be used to illustrate all of those who lost horses from the area. The owner of the company, William Rouse, kept two of the horses, Tommy and Billy, in a field that today is Whatcombe Road, in Frome. When they were not working the horses would graze in the field and became a familiar sight to passers by, trotting over to 'greet' many of them. During the summers the horses would accompany the Rouse family on picnics to nearby Orchardleigh Lake. While William, his wife and two children travelled in a four-seater gig, Tommy and Billy would be ridden by brothers Bernard and Hubert Browne, friends of the family but both known affectionately as 'uncle'. The warm summer of 1914, with its seemingly endless idyllic sunny afternoons, had been no different.

With the onset of war, however, Tommy and Billy, along with another of Mr Rouse's horses, were commandeered. His children, Doreen and Thomas, would later relate the sadness of the day the horses were collected and taken by the army for training, before no doubt going across to the Western Front.

The two 'uncles' enlisted and a few months into the war, Bernard, serving with the Army Medical Corps, was assembled for inspection and about to be addressed by one of the officers. As the mounted officer moved along the line his horse began to nay and turned his head toward Bernard. The officer then spoke saying: 'This horse seems to know you.' Indeed the horse did, as it was Tommy and later that day Bernard visited his old friend, no doubt recounting some of the many times he had ridden him back in Frome. Three days later, both Tommy and the officer were killed in action. Billy and the third horse were never heard of again and so it can be assumed they met the same fate.

The strong bond between man and horse that

Bernard Browne.

Many horses were born on the Western Front during the conflict.

could develop was understood by the army and so adverts appeared calling for men to join the Army Remount Department. Although the age range of those required was between twenty-five and forty, the overriding prerequisite, as capitalised in bold letters on the advert, was: 'ONLY MEN THOROUGLY ACCUSTOMED TO HORSES REQUIRED'. It was not only the Remount Department that required these kind of men, as each regiment or army unit needed to look after their horses once they had been transferred to them.

One of those tasked with looking after horses was Driver Ernie Brooks, who before the war had worked for E.J. Hoddinott at Witham Hall Farm. In the letter to his former employer where he had described being shelled on Christmas Day, Ernie also gave an insight into what life was like for men and horses on the frontlines.

'The weather is cold again. We have had a slight snowstorm,
and there appears a lot more ready to fall. There is nothing but
mud about. All the pastureland is knee deep in mud, and it is
made worse by the horses that are picketed and by the guns and
wagon. My own horses are still in working order, but I have one
with only one eye. He lost an eye at B - - - - - after the Battle of
Mons. We turned in pursuit of the enemy and drove them back
to the Aisne, where we came in action at B - - - - - and our battery
was cut up. We lost 17 men killed and some wounded and we
also lost 34 horses. My other horse had a narrow escape. A piece
of shell about 12lbs ripped the rear of my saddle out. Anyhow, I
got them out of that and I still have both in working order. Then
we fought our way up to Armentieres and Nieppe and so on, but
I must not go any further or this letter won't pass.'

As the amount of dead horses increased the government had to replace them, but as the number required could simply not be met by the home market, the government had to look elsewhere to satisfy their requirement – across the Atlantic.

If a shortage of horses was one problem the army constantly had to solve, then a lack of artillery shells, as highlighted at Neuve Chapelle, was even more pressing. This shortage would lead to the 'Shell Scandal' of May 1915 and ultimately bring the government down. Around the country many companies switched from their peace-time businesses to manufacturing munitions. In Frome, several firms were involved in this work.

One of those companies, making shell casings for the army, was J.W. Singer & Sons Ltd. The founder of the company, John Webb Singer, had been born in Frome almost a century before. During his youth he watched with enthusiasm the goings on at a foundry near where he lived at the Butts. Although he had tried casting toy cannons, it was not until much later he established his boyhood passion as a full-time business. After leaving school he had undertaken an apprenticeship in a local watchmaker firm. On completing this, he went to work in London, but later returned to manage the Frome business. At the same time, he began a sideline of making brass ornaments for local churches, for which the rise of the Oxford Movement within the Church of England and its avocation to reinstate some of the older Christian traditions of faith had created a large demand. Eventually establishing an art metal work foundry and giving up watch-making, J.W. Singer saw his new business grow and expand, so establishing the firm as a major employer in the town and culminating in its becoming a limited company at the tail-end of the nineteenth century. The bronze statues cast during this period of time included iconic ones such as 'Boudica and Her Daughters', which stands on the Thames

The casting of 'Boudica and Her Daughters' at J.W. Singer's foundry, 1902.

Embankment, 'Lady Justice' on the dome above the Old Bailey and 'Alfred the Great' at Winchester. The firm's work was also exported to countries including Australia, India, South Africa and New Zealand, as well as being displayed at exhibitions in London and Paris.

On J.W. Singer's death in 1904, his two sons, Herbert and Edgar, continued the business, having taken it over around the time the company became limited. By the outbreak of the First World War though, the firm was experiencing financial difficulties, mainly due to its capital structure. In the short term an amalgamation with their major rivals, the Birmingham firm Spital & Clark, eased these worries slightly, although it might not be too much of an overstatement to say the company's fortunes were turned around by the war.

Once hostilities had started, the company was requisitioned by the Government and its workforce converted to munitions manufacture. The nearby Market Hall was used as a foundry for making the shell cases, along with fuses. During the period of the First World War more than 700 people were employed by the firm in this work. Paradoxically,

A seismic change in employment took place during the war; women were employed in traditionally male jobs for the first time.

as the war had increased its financial stability, it had, at the same time, depleted its workforce; with former employees having either been called up as reservists or else enlisting. With such a shortfall and not enough men to replace them, women were employed for the first time in the company's history. This in itself reflects another huge change the war forced onto the local population – that of women taking on jobs traditionally the reserve of men.

The hours were long, the environment dirty and noisy and the factory could be a dangerous place to work. One employee, for example, lost all the fingers on her right hand in a circular saw accident, while the next year a new employee had a finger severed, on her very first morning, by a stamping machine she was being trained on.

A more traditional role for women, perhaps, but no less important.

An occupation more traditionally associated with women was nursing and the need for hospitals and staff, once the wounded began coming back to England, became as great as anything else in supporting the war effort. As early as Friday, 7 August 1914, the *Somerset and Wilts Journal* reported that preparations were being made for the reception of the wounded, should the occasion arise. Sixty beds would be provided, the newspaper said, and the town had been already canvassed for the purpose of obtaining promises of equipment and supplies to help run a temporary hospital, along with suitable premises for it. Initially the Market Hall in the town centre had been earmarked for conversion to a hospital, but as mentioned in the previous section, this would become instead a munitions factory for J.W. Singer & Sons Ltd.

An embroidered postcard depicting the British Red Cross emblem.

In the end, two other buildings in Frome were chosen, both of which would be officially recognised as Red Cross Auxiliary Hospitals: these were St Aldhelm's Home for Boys and Keyford Asylum. In the introduction to the booklet recording a list of the 3,000 or so Auxiliary Hospitals that existed during the First World War, its author had the following to say:

> '*At the outbreak of the First World War the British Red Cross and the Order of St John of Jerusalem combined to form the joint war committee. They pooled their resources under the protection of the Red Cross emblem. As the Red Cross had secured buildings, equipment and staff, the organisation was able to set up temporary hospitals as soon as wounded men began to arrive back in England. The buildings varied widely, ranging from town halls and schools, to large and small private houses, both in the country and in cities, the most suitable ones were established as auxiliary hospitals.* [These] *were attached to central Military Hospitals, which looked after patients who remained under military control.*
>
> *There were over 3,000 auxiliary hospitals administered by Red Cross county directors. In many cases, women in the local neighbourhood volunteered on a part-time basis. The hospital often needed to supplement voluntary work with paid-roles, such as cooks. Local medics also volunteered, despite the extra strain that the medical profession was already under at that time. The patients of these hospitals were generally less seriously wounded than at other hospitals and they needed to convalesce. The serviceman preferred the auxiliary hospitals to military hospitals because they were not so strict, they were less crowded and the surroundings were more homely.*'

As mentioned, there were two auxiliary hospitals in Frome itself (a third was at nearby Longleat House, but this will be covered in a later chapter). The first, St Aldhelm's Home for Boys, became a hospital for only part of the war. The 'Home' came into being through the *Church of England Incorporated Society for providing Homes for Waifs and*

Strays. Initially located elsewhere in the town, it moved to its new home on the corner of Green Lane and Oakfield Road in 1887. It was one of thirty homes the Society had around the country providing such a service, and the forty-two boys it accommodated in Frome were educated in various trades, especially printing. It had its own printing press called, perhaps unsurprisingly, the St Aldhelm's Press. When the building was taken over by the Red Cross, temporarily as it transpired, the boys moved out to other homes.

A more permanent auxiliary hospital was established at Keyford Asylum, which stood on what is today the corner of Culverhill and Stevens Lane (the building was demolished in 1956). The Asylum was built through an endowment by a man called Richard Stevens. Along with his brother, John, he had already endowed a number of pupils at a similar building located in the middle of Frome. But whereas this centre-based Charity School, known as the Blue House, catered for the education of young boys, along with twenty widows from the town who had been selected to live in the adjoining almshouse, the new building in Keyford (a once separate settlement to the south-east of the town centre) was established to accommodate old men and young girls who were trained for domestic service. To cater for the needs of the

Keyford Asylum first opened its doors in 1804.

Residents of the Asylum before the war, although the men's establishment was officially known as Keyford Hospital.

old men though, a hospital had already been established at the Asylum, so when war broke out and suitable buildings were sought, it became an obvious choice.

Like the majority of Red Cross auxiliary hospitals across the country, it was staffed mainly by women from the Voluntary Aid Detachment (VAD). This was an organisation that provided field nursing services in hospitals in Britain and countries within its Empire. The VAD system was founded in 1909, with the help of the Red Cross and the Order of St John, and by summer 1914 more than 2,500 Voluntary Aid Detachments units existed nationally, including one in Frome. The majority of the 74,000 volunteers countrywide were female and usually members of the middle to upper classes. Initially treated suspiciously or with contempt by trained nurses at the start of the war, these VAD nurses nevertheless acquitted themselves admirably during it and eventually gained the respect of their colleagues.

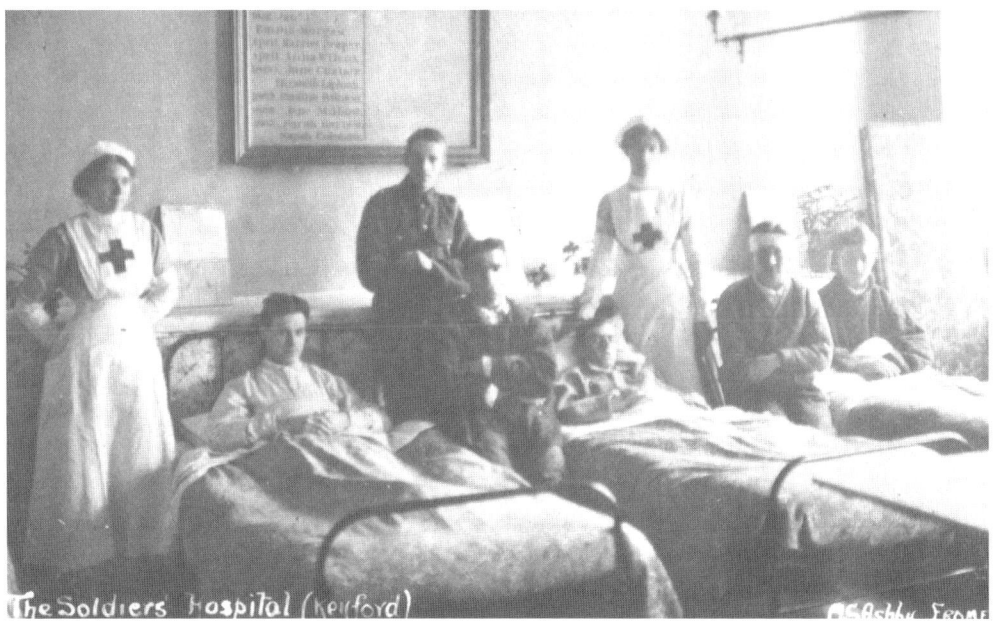

A number of the wounded soldiers who benefited from the Asylum's role as a military hospital during the First World War.

Each local VAD had a Commandant in charge and in Frome this was Miss Curwen. The branch's Vice-President was Lady Kathleen Thynne, whose family owned the Longleat Estate. From the very beginning the members of the local VAD took on the responsibility of organising hospital beds and provisions; in fact they were the ones the *Journal* reported had canvassed the local businesses and individuals for equipment, supplies and possible premises.

Once the Red Cross Hospital at Keyford was operational, a host of other local volunteers and organisations contributed in various ways. One example was the Frome Fanciers Association, who organized collections of fresh eggs for hospital patients. So successful was this, they not only fulfilled local needs but were able to contribute large numbers to the national egg collection headquarters in London. So much so that they were eventually recognised by the War Office as the local authorized depot.

Another vital organisation in supporting the work of Keyford Hospital opened in October 1915, in Cheap Street, and was called the Frome War Hospital Supply Depot. A notice appeared in the 10 September 1914 issue of the *Somerset Standard* which stated:

'It has been thought it might prove helpful to those in the neighbourhood who are anxious to work for Hospitals and for soldiers in the field if a work depot were started in Frome on the same lines as those which have proved so useful in other towns in stimulating the output of work.'

The notice went on to say that it was hoped to take a house in Frome which would be open for work daily from 11am to 5pm.

The 'house' they found was at No.2 Cheap Street and was provided rent free by its owner, Mr Beauchamp. The premises were quickly divided into several main workrooms, with volunteers working in each between 11am and 1pm and then again between 2pm and 5pm. An exception was the carpenter's 'shop', which opened in the evening, as most of the male volunteers worked elsewhere during the day. Once there, the men would make all manner of aids, such as leg rests, crutches and splints.

Another workroom at the Frome War Hospital Supply Depot was used for sewing. The items made here ranged from bandages, shell dressings and anti-vermin vests, to swabs, stretcher quilts and theatre towels. One woman who answered an appeal for volunteer workers was Doreen Rouse, whose father, William, owned the Selwood Wagon Works. She would later remember the great sense of urgency in the workroom as they sewed and also the terrible sadness whenever news of a Frome 'lad' having been killed was received at the depot.

Doreen Rouse, one of many local people who volunteered to work at the Frome War Hospital Supply Depot.

During the first couple of months of its opening, this sadness would envelope the depot many times, as they learnt of the deaths of such Frome 'lads' as Albert Webley, a private in the Royal Medical Corps who had worked for local firm Wilson & Co of Welshmill before the war and died on 21 October 1915 in Mesopotamia, Witham Friary born Percy Hughes, a Royal Field Artillery gunner who died on 23 October

QUEEN MARY'S NEEDLEWORK GUILD.

BADGE CERTIFICATE.

Miss D. Rouse.

of _Selwood Terrace. Vallis way Frome._

having been engaged in voluntary war work for the Q.M.N.G. has been granted the badge of the Guild, which she is entitled to wear during the war, so long as she continues a voluntary worker.

ST. JAMES'S PALACE.

Annie Lawley

Hon. Sec.

Date _30ᵗʰ March 1916_.

The certificate of the Queen Mary's Needlework Guild which entitled its holder to wear the badge of the Guild.

The Queen Mary's Needlework Guild badge.

when his transport ship was torpedoed, and Somerset Light Infantryman George Duck, who had been in charge of Frome railway station bookstore in the three years prior to enlisting.

This great sense of loss would hang like a dark cloud over the rest of Frome as well and for the second year running, many families would have to endure a Christmas without loved ones being still alive.

An editorial in the _Somerset Standard_ dated 31 December 1915, reflected on the mood which had prevailed during the festive period:

'_The sorrows of a great war and the dreariness of the weather exerted a chastening influence_ *on the spirit of Christmas, and the people were in a somewhat subdued mood. Before the Kaiser and his wicked advisers disturbed the peace of Europe and produced much suffering in the world, Christmas was a time for rejoicing – a time when the heart responded merrily to gladsome surroundings and happy associations, but for the second year the festival has been robbed of its joyousness, and one had to look for the religious meaning of the message of 'glad tidings of great joy'. Still, if the people have not been boisterously happy, the festival has been peacefully spent in the quiet repose of the homes.'*

As for those on the front lines, the *Standard* reported that:

'Christmas Day broke over the British Western Front wet, blowing and altogether cheerless. As the morning advanced, however, the clouds began to roll up and take a paler hue, the sun struggled through in a misty, rayless manner, and by dinnertime (that is to say the soldiers' dinnertime) it was quite fine, and best of all, very mild. On the whole, as far I have been able to learn, the day has been a pretty uneventful one in the trenches. Plenty of good fare was provided, and the conditions were as comfortable as it was possible to render them amid the waterlogged environment, which no degree of effort has proved equal to overcoming successfully. Amongst the troops in reserve and in billets Christmas was of course celebrated with far more traditional thoroughness.'

With the approach of a second winter the British armed forces settled into the now familiar routine of troop rotation, at least in front line trenches, to avoid men becoming complacent. No group of soldiers occupied the same section of trench for more than a month or so before they were moved either up or down 'The Line'. Short bursts of intense excitement – perhaps a raid, or counter-attack – relieved the otherwise tedious periods of boredom punctuated nevertheless by attritional losses to snipers or shell fire. One highlight, however, saw leave now being granted to men who had served in France and Flanders. For many, they had not been home for nearly eighteen months.

One of those given leave was Lance Corporal Edwin Thomas Udell of the 6th Battalion Gloucestershire Regiment. A gardener in pre-war Frome he had been employed at Welshmill House by Miss Sinkins and Fromefield House by the Reverend Gordon, among other places. In early December 1915 he came home to Frome on three weeks leave, no doubt staying at his parent's house in Leys Lane. A few days after returning to the Western Front, on Christmas Day afternoon, he was killed by a German shell which landed in the trench he was occupying.

The Somerset Standard *editorial looks back on the year of 1915.*

CHAPTER 5

The Realization (Jan–Dec 1916)

By the end of 1915 it was estimated that almost two and half million men had volunteered to fight during the seventeen months the First World War had been raging. However, given the unprecedented numbers of dead and wounded the war had produced, it was not enough. Despite the great pressure put on men to get them into khaki – Lord Kitchener's famous 'Your Country Needs You' poster, girls handing over white feathers and clergymen using their sermons to urge men to enlist, among many examples – it was discovered in August 1915 that two million men of military age had not yet volunteered.

A plan called The Group Scheme, although probably better known as the Derby Scheme, after its originator Lord Derby who was in charge of recruiting, was subsequently launched. In this programme, eligible married men, along with single ones, were encouraged to register for military duty on the understanding that married men would only be required when all of the single men on the register had been called up. It became a short lived scheme, mainly due to the fact very few single men came forward to register, meaning the large number of married men who had done so were called up almost immediately and sent off to fight.

The demise of the Derby Scheme ultimately led to the Military Service Act or conscription. The bill was approved in January –

SiR JOHN & LADY BARLOW & FAMILY, COLWYN BAY, JULY 6 19

John Barlow was Member of Parliament for Frome between 1892 and 1895. He regained his seat the following year and remained in power until he was ousted in the first post-war election.

although controversially Frome MP Sir John Barlow, a Quaker and pacifist, voted against it – and came into effect two months later, on 2 March 1916. The Act required all single males of British nationality between the ages of eighteen and forty-one to undertake compulsory service in the armed forces. Within three months this was expanded to include all married men in that age group and by the end of the war, the upper age limit would stand at fifty.

For those in the Frome district, as elsewhere, men could become exempt for service if the work they were engaged in was deemed to be of national importance. Being the sole supporter of dependants, medically unfit or being a conscientious objector were other ways to be certified exempt. For those wishing to obtain this certification, however, they had to appear before a tribunal.

When Frome building contractor Arthur Barnes appeared before a tribunal he requested exemption on the grounds that he was sole proprietor and manager of one of the oldest building firms in Frome and for the previous fourteen months his company had been undertaking extensions and alterations for other firms employed on government work, with several of these contracts still to be completed and others waiting to commence. On top of this, Barnes, of Locks Hill, told the tribunal that he had an invalid wife and three children as dependants. To have to go and serve would be his ruin, he declared, as there was no one to take over from him. To reinforce his case, the clerk read a letter from the captain of the local Fire Brigade, in which Arthur Barnes was a senior fireman, stating that since the beginning of the war the brigade's strength had been halved through members joining up and it would be 'courting trouble' if any more were taken. The upshot of all this overwhelming 'evidence' was that the military representative assented that if the tribunal were satisfied, then conditional exemption should be granted.

Others, however, were given only temporary reprieve. T.C. Davy, for example, at the time caretaker of Frome public baths, was given exemption until the end of the bathing season, which was due to finish in September.

Still more eligible men aimed to seek exemption through being conscientious objectors. The proprietor of a Frome general business store in Palmer Street, E.J. Holloway, appeared before the tribunal and appealed to its members by citing three reasons to exempt him: that he was a conscientious objector to military service, if called up he would lose his business and that he was in poor health. This appeal was also successful, although the chairman, rather sardonically perhaps, hoped his health would improve along with his conscience.

For those seeking exemption solely on the 'conscientious objector' ticket the tribunal members could be a lot tougher, depending on what sort of objector they were dealing with. There were two types: Alternatives and Absolutists. The Alternatives did not want to be responsible for shedding any blood, but were prepared to serve in non-combatant roles which many subsequently did with distinction. The Absolutists were a much more troublesome group for the tribunals. The line of questioning used on this group was intended to get them to admit that under certain circumstances they would resort to violence, leaving them with no real case for exemption. 'What would you do if a criminal assaulted your mother?' and 'What would you do if a stranger attempted to rape your wife?' were two such examples. Alternatively, questions were aimed at undermining their 'conscience' argument. These might include the following: 'If you saw children dying in the wreckage caused by an air raid would you help them?' or 'Would you leave a man suffering from wounds to die, because to help him would be against your conscience?' One man, in neighbouring Bath, that answered affirmative to both the above questions also stated

L'embusqué délaissé,
The slacker slighted.

One of many postcards portraying scenes in which girls were seen to prefer the company of men in uniform to those in civilian clothing, or so called 'slackers'.

that he would not help a wounded soldier on crutches if he fell in the street in front of him. Nevertheless, he was denied exemption and in the subsequent period of time before going off to serve, was subjected to increasing hostility from neighbours, culminating in the burning of a life-size effigy, complete with a card strapped across the chest inscribed: 'The man who would not help a Zeppelin victim.'

It eventually reached the point where anyone still in civilian attire, but not visibly infirm, was likely to be deemed a 'shirker', 'lagger', 'slacker' or, worst of all, a 'conchie', a derogatory term used for conscientious objectors. There were a number of ways to tell if someone had enlisted but was still waiting to do their duty though, or had already answered the call but been honourably discharged. The former, at least during the Derby Scheme, saw men who had registered to join the army but were waiting for their call up wearing khaki armbands with a red crown, while those honourably discharged, usually through being wounded, wore the Silver War Badge.

Determined to induct as many men as possible into the armed services police forces were instructed to attended theatres, music halls and football matches to question those not in uniform. Once 'apprehended' the men had to produce the relevant documentation or registration card to prove exemption from military service or else explain why they were still in civilian clothing. In 1917 when the circus came to Frome the local police force was there in numbers. Despite this, however, they did not apprehend one slacker, shirker, lagger or even conchie.

During the Derby Scheme, there were also many local men who volunteered to join the navy (the khaki armband of those registered but still waiting call-up emblazoned with a blue crown) so joining the vast number of their fellows from the Frome area already serving at sea, many of whom had made careers of it.

At the beginning of the twentieth century the Royal Navy's dominance of the high seas had been in place for centuries, defending its country's interests all around the globe. Indeed, its superiority had been the foundation on which the British Empire was able to expand to the point where it was said the 'sun never set upon it' and within its history there was such celebrated victories as the defeat of the Spanish Armada, along with the battles of the Nile and Trafalgar. In the years leading up to the First World War though, this superiority had been seriously challenged by Germany. So much so that an intense rivalry had developed to see who could build the biggest vessel. This turned out to be a new type of battleship that ushered in what became known as the Age of the Dreadnought, named after the first of these huge ironclad ships: HMS *Dreadnought*. At the beginning of hostilities, in August 1914, Britain still held the balance of power, with twenty dreadnoughts compared to Germany's thirteen with the other classes of ships in the British Fleet being almost double in number of their rival.

Despite the supremacy of the Royal Navy, the British did not seek a major engagement – the Germans were like-minded – as each battleship cost so much to build they did not want to risk it being sunk. Only one major naval battle took place throughout the war, the Battle of Jutland.

Throughout the war the British Grand Fleet was based in the Orkney Islands, at Scapa Flow, although there were also major naval bases at

HMS Dreadnought. *Launched in 1906 it was the first of its kind. So revolutionary was this battleship, it gave its name to a new type of ship and made everything before it as good as obsolete.*

Chatham, Plymouth, Portsmouth and Rosyth. In addition, there were squadrons of British warships scattered across the oceans of the world, with many men from the Frome area serving on board these ships. Although there was no major engagement until this year that is not to say the British had not suffered losses to their fleet. The nature of the war until 1916 had been a tactical one of hit and run; small forces attacking quickly and inflicting as much damage as possible on enemy shipping. Sometimes there was as little as one vessel inflicting this damage. These were usually submarines or, in the case of the German navy, the U-boat. Throughout the war these submersibles would inflict untold damage and take countless lives, both servicemen and civilians, many of the former being from Frome and its environs.

The war was less than two months old when three British armoured cruisers HMS *Aboukir*, HMS *Hogue* and HMS *Cressy* were sunk by a lone U-boat. On board the *Cressy* was Able Seaman William Turner, aged 49, who was originally from Frome and became the town's first naval casualty.

HMS *Cressy*, like the other two cruisers, had been built around the turn of the century. The trio of ships had been cruising off the Dutch coast. As they were slow in speed and manoeuvring power, it was therefore work for which they were not really suited and so made easy targets. Nevertheless, it was a case of 'needs must' and they found themselves patrolling the North Sea to guard against raids on the Belgian coast and to protect British transport ships.

HMS *Aboukir* was the first to be hit by one of the U-boat's torpedoes. Although thinking her sister ship had hit a mine, HMS *Cressy* steered a course to rescue the men on board. As the *Cressy* did this, so HMS *Hogue* was hit as well. This second cruiser stayed afloat for around twenty minutes before it sank. HMS *Cressy* now had the task of trying to rescue men from both ships but before she could go any further, she herself was hit by a torpedo. The ship turned upside down and in no time at all had also sunk. In total 62 officers and 1,400 men were lost across all three British cruisers. Of these, 536 men, including 25 officers, were from the *Cressy*. Able Seaman William Turner was one of them. He was the son of William Turner, of Frome, but had moved to live in Holloway, London, where he now left a widow.

It wasn't always the German navy that inflicted damage upon British ships, however. As mentioned in an earlier chapter, HMS *Bulwark*, anchored off Sheerness, suffered an internal explosion which killed, among hundreds of others, Private William Stillman and 18-year-old Seaman William Wheeler, of Egford Bottom, Frome.

In May 1916 the Battle of Jutland occurred. It had not been intended as a major engagement of the opposing fleets, but rather a game of cat and mouse between two smaller naval forces. According to David Evans in *The First World War*:

William Wheeler was only 18 years old when he was killed on 26 November 1914. Serving as a Boy 1st Class on HMS Bulwark *for the previous eighteen months, he had joined the navy in 1912.*

> *'The German plan was to bait a trap and tempt Admiral Beatty's battle cruiser squadron out of Rosyth in the belief that it was chasing a relatively small German force. Von Hipper, the commander of the German squadron, would then retire with Beatty in hot pursuit and so draw him unwittingly towards the main German fleet that was some 80 kilometres (50 miles) distant over the horizon. Beatty's ships would then be easily overwhelmed.'*

What the German navy did not know, however, was that the British knew exactly what was being planned, through access to their secret codes, and were in the process of planning their own trap along similar lines. What this meant in practice, was that the majority of the British Grand Fleet put to sea alongside Beatty, although they remained out of sight. It was not long before the two squadrons – that of Beatty and von Hipper – came into view of each other. Admiral von Hipper then withdrew, so initiating his 'trap'. What happened next is described by David Evans:

> *'During the long-range duel that followed, the Royal Navy lost two battleships, but von Hipper and his squadron found themselves in difficulty and so the order was given from the*

HMS Invincible. *Sunk at the Battle of Jutland, on 31 May 1916, when enemy ships landed several direct salvos side on. More than 1,000 officers and men perished.*

German High Seas Fleet to enter the affray. Once this happened, the British Grand Fleet, commanded by Admiral Jellicoe, did the same; the result being that the two main fleets now faced each other.'

The British quickly gained the upper hand and might have secured a famous victory, but Admiral Scheer, in charge of the German fleet, ordered a hasty withdrawal. Fighting did resume later and the British again held the upper hand, Admiral Jellicoe this time cutting off the German navy's means of retreat. With night descending and dense smoke all around, however, Admiral Scheer's fleet was able to break through the British line and get safely back to port. The only major naval battle of the war was over. Although each side would claim victory, both fleets suffered heavily in terms of tonnage sunk. On the British side the most devastating loss was the trio of battlecruisers, HMS *Indefatigable*, HMS *Invincible* and HMS *Queen Mary*. All experienced huge explosions after direct hits and sank in a matter of minutes.

As for the Frome men who took part in the battle, there were ten fatalities, four of which were aboard the *Indefatigable*. They were Stoker 1st Class Frederick Coombs, of Beckington and Stoker 1st Class William Applegate from Buckland Dinham, along with Electrician 4th Class Arthur 'Art' Richards and Able Seaman Nelson Topp, both from Frome. The *Indefatigable* had been the rear cruiser in the battle fleet

HMS Queen Mary. *Along with HMS* Invincible, *this 27,000 ton battle cruiser was sunk at the Battle of Jutland at the cost of more than 1,000 men, including Able Seaman William Keen from Frome.*

and so had come in for a particular pounding when German guns had concentrated on her. Under this massed firepower she keeled over and once her bottom was blown out, she sank. Nearly 800 personnel died.

The others from Frome who were killed on that day, 31 May 1916: were Engine Room Artificer 3rd Class Alfred Malcolm and Private Albert Charlton of the Royal Marine Light Infantry, both aboard HMS *Invincible*; Able Seaman William Keen serving on HMS *Queen Mary*; Stokers 1st Class Nelson Benger and Arthur Wheeler on board HMS *Broke* and HMS *Warrior* respectively, and Chief Stoker John Sparrow.

On 5 June 1916, two more Frome men were killed. They were both on board HMS *Hampshire* when it hit a mine off the Orkney Islands and sank. The ship had taken part in the Battle of

Able Seaman Nelson Topp was serving on HMS Indefatigable *when he was killed at the Battle of Jutland. He is commemorated on the Plymouth Naval Memorial and Frome War Memorial.*

Stoker Arthur Wheeler was killed at the Battle of Jutland, while serving on HMS Warrior. *Before the war he had worked for Great Western Railway, but had enlisted in the navy in June 1915.*

Bugler William Wheeler was only 16 years old when he was killed in June 1916. He was on board HMS Hampshire, *on a secret mission to Russia, with Lord Kitchener and his staff when the cruiser hit a mine and quickly sank.*

Along with William Wheeler, Private Ivor Edwards was aboard HMS Hampshire, *with Lord Kitchener and his staff, when it sank, taking with it more than 700 lives. He was only 18.*

Jutland the previous week but had come through unscathed. On this particular day the ship was taking Lord Kitchener and his staff on a secret mission to Russia. Bugler William Wheeler, aged 16, and Private Ivor Edwards, aged 18, both of the Royal Marine Light Infantry, were the two local men killed. More than 700 other lives were also lost.

Another piece of legislation that came into being in 1916, alongside conscription, concerned natural light. Daylight Saving Time was introduced in Britain in May of that year so as to minimize use of artificial lighting and thus save fuel for the war effort. Germany had implemented it the previous month and Britain quickly followed suit.

In the same month as the Battle of Jutland and the introduction of Daylight Saving Time, the first edition of *The Longleat Lyre* was issued. This was a monthly magazine produced for the staff and patients at the Military Relief Hospital located at the Longleat Estate, in Wiltshire.

Longleat House was built in the sixteenth century, on the site of a former priory, by Sir John Thynne the younger, the first of the Thynne dynasty who would live in the stately home. His descendents later attained the peerage title of Marquess of Bath, along with the subsidiary titles of Viscount Weymouth and Baron Thynne of Warminster. From earliest times the Thynne family had connections with Frome, as they

Longleat House, the residence of the Thynne family.

were involved in many of its affairs, such as the appointment of Frome vicars and representing the town as its Member of Parliament.

Thomas Henry Thynne, Viscount Weymouth from birth and later the 5th Marquess of Bath, represented Frome as its MP for six years, between 1886 and 1892, and then again from 1895. In the following year, 1896, his father died and he inherited the Marquisate and moved to the House of Lords. As Lord Bath he became a lieutenant colonel of the Royal Wiltshire Yeomanry, as well as an honorary colonel of that regiment and of the 4th Battalion of the Somerset Light Infantry. He married Violet Caroline Mordaunt and they had five children: Alice Kathleen, Emma, John, Mary and Henry. By the time of the inaugural issue of

Second Lieutenant John Alexander Thynne, also known as Viscount Weymouth.

The Longleat Lyre in May 1916, one of the boys had died in the war – Second Lieutenant John Alexander Thynne, aged 20, of the Royal Scots Greys, who had been killed in action on 13 February 1916.

In this initial copy of *The Longleat Lyre* Lady Bath gave a fascinating account into how the hospital had started, detailing just how much hard effort had gone on behind the scenes to turn their stately home into a place of healing. She recounted:

> *'I think it was when we heard of all the wounded trooping home after the retreat from Mons, that Lord Bath and I felt that we ought to make this big house of use to the nation.'*

The intention was to turn Longleat House and its extensive grounds into a convalescent home for officers. Lord Bath duly wrote to the War Office at the end of August with the offer and a week later Doctor Barton arrived to inspect the rooms for suitability:

> '[Doctor Barton] *went all over them and said they were most suitable and would do very well. He also asked me many*

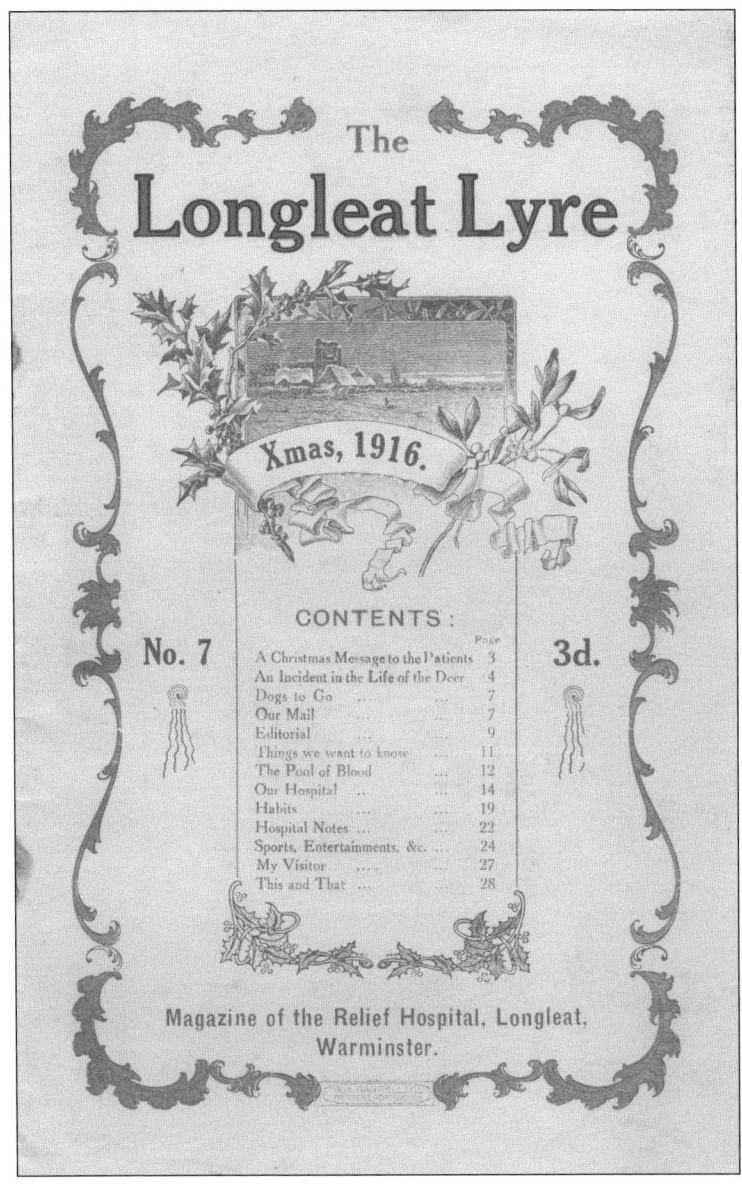

The Longleat Lyre *was a monthly magazine for staff and patients of the hospital, although it was on sale in several places in Frome. This is the Christmas edition for 1916, which had a colour cover. It is numbered No.7, but sequentially is actually No.8.*

questions concerning the purity of the water, the climate, the water supply, the distance from the station, and by what means patients could be conveyed from the station, if we had an ambulance, or if one could be obtained, if wanted, and if we had any objection to surgical cases, as some ladies minded the sight of bandages. I said: "No, we were not in the least afraid, and only wanted to do what was of most use."

He then turned to me and said, "Well, Lady Bath, if you don't mind my saying so, it would be far more useful if you could have a hospital for Tommies, instead of a convalescent home for Officers." I asked him "Why?" He answered, "Because if every single officer we have at present in the British Army were to fall sick tomorrow, I would have about three beds apiece to offer them, whereas we are sadly in need of beds for our Tommies, and they are such splendid fellows, I don't believe you would find them a very great deal of trouble to look after or to keep in order."'

After consulting with her husband it was agreed Longleat would receive 'Tommies' instead of officers. It was then, as Lady Bath describes it, the hard work really began. All furniture, including large cupboards and four poster beds, had to be taken out of the rooms now set aside as wards and storage space found elsewhere in the house. Curtains had to be taken down and carpets rolled up, while the current occupants had to vacate their rooms. Lady Emma's room, for example, was to become No.1 ward, while those of her brother, Lord Henry and sister, Lady Mary, were to become wards No.2 and No.9 respectively. Wards No.4 through to No.6 had previously been visitors' bedrooms. A week later, with the rooms empty, they began to be refurnished, this time with around thirty beds. Two thirds of the beds were obtained from around the house, while the remaining third were purchased out of the estate's own money.

Once the new hospital was ready the authorities were notified. However, a long wait occurred and nothing happened. Eventually it was discovered the cause of the delay was through the use of the term 'convalescent home' and if willing to change it to a 'Military Relief

Hospital', the stately home could begin to receive patients immediately. Once more there was agreement to the change.

As it turned out, there was still much more to do before they were truly ready, but once the nurses began to arrive, their experience revealed what was needed.

'The next morning Sister Disney arrived in my sitting-room looking very business-like in her veil and apron, with her note-book in her hand. "Good morning, Lady Bath! I have had a look round the hospital and I am afraid I have found a great many things wanting!" I said "Really Sister," and I know that I must have looked surprised, because I thought that we had got everything, but then you see I had never furnished a hospital before! Sister Disney then took up her list and started on the chief item, which was the linen. She asked me how much we had, and I was glad to be able to produce a list of the most important items, such as sheets, pillow-slips, towels etc, but after a conversation with Mrs Parker, we found that there still a good many things to buy, such as bath-towels, round-towels, dusters, and cloths of all kinds, because, of course, it must be remembered, that although we could spare the sheets, pillow-slips and ordinary towels, which had been used by our visitors, all cloths and dusters which we had were still needed for the part of the house which was not used for the hospital, but we found that the bulk of the linen could be produced out of Mrs Parker's well-kept linen cupboard.

The linen having been gone through and settled, Sister Disney read out the rest of the list. It consisted of the following articles: enamel basins of many shapes and sizes, pails, zinc corn-bins to be used as dirty clothes baskets, sanitary dustbins, hair-brushes, combs, nail-brushes, tooth-brushes, slippers, dressing-gowns, pyjamas, night-shirts, socks, doctors' linen coats and overalls, stock drugs, disinfectant and bandages of all sorts, shapes and sizes.'

A few of the patients who came through the doors of Longleat during its time as a relief hospital.

Some of the doctors and nurses who worked at the relief hospital.

The upshot of this was that Lady Kathleen and a Nurse Kent went into Frome to get the supplies, some of which – the bandages and garments for example – were provided by the local branch of the British Red Cross Society. They also provided several Voluntary Aid Detachment nurses to work at Longleat. Once everything was actually ready, the relief hospital opened its doors with twelve rooms and thirty-one beds. There was some confusion as to whether the first assignment of patients would be English or Belgian, but when the vehicles conveying the soldiers from Frome railway station to the house pulled up on the driveway, they were found to be Belgian soldiers.

Although 1914 had been bad in terms of the loss of life of Frome men, mostly occurring on the Western Front, and 1915 subsequently worse, in many ways both of these paled into insignificance when compared to the mass slaughter that is now associated with 1916. In one month alone that year – July – more men from the Frome area were killed in action than all those who died in 1914 put together (albeit only the final five months of the year). But it is hardly surprising, as this particular month saw the beginning of the most infamous of all the battles associated with the First World War: the Battle of the Somme.

At the beginning of 1916 both British and German high commands were in the process of putting the final touches to their strategies for the coming year. The Germans had decided to attempt the capture of the French city of Verdun, which was seen as an important and strategic base. It was surrounded by an impressive array of fortresses and the Germans knew that if the city fell it would be a huge blow to French morale and so would be defended at any cost.

The British, meanwhile, led by their new commander-in-chief Sir Douglas Haig, had decided their offensive would take place along a 17-mile stretch of land which ran through a valley and alongside a nearby river. Both gave their name to the battle: Somme. Haig had actually wanted to attack later in the year, but due to the pressure on the French at Verdun he brought his plans forward and so the offensive began on 1 July 1916. This date has gone down in the annals of history as one of the most merciless and blackest days in the history of the British Army.

On that initial day alone there were around 60,000 British casualties, nearly a third being fatalities and many of them were men from Frome

British soldiers during the Somme campaign.

and the surrounding areas. These included Privates Charles Lee, Thomas Dredge and Charles Gamble, Sergeants Albert Parsons and Stanley Hansford and Lance Corporal John Lewer. All of these soldiers were serving in various battalions of the Somerset Regiment and most were to have no known grave. The Battle of the Somme lasted five months and in that period of time the number of men killed from the area remained high.

It wasn't just on the Western Front that saw the lives of Frome men so cruelly extinguished that month, however. For example, both Private Bertie Hobbs of the Hampshire Regiment and Private Harold Phillips serving with the 1/4 Somersets died in Mesopotamia, the latter from disease.

Private Charles Lee was killed on the first day of the Somme. His mother, of Vicarage Street, Frome, initially learned of his death through a letter received from a comrade of her son.

In September came the death of another soldier killed in action at the Somme. This was Lieutenant Raymond Asquith of the 3rd Battalion Grenadier Guards, the son of the current British Prime Minister and son-in-law to the Horners of Mells. He was a frequent visit to the village of Mells and his wife and children were actually staying there when they received news of his death.

With the end of the Somme offensive in November 1916, the numbers of men dying reduced drastically, to the point where the only soldier from the Frome area to die in December was Mells-born Frank Phillips, who was a 45-year-old sapper with the 4th Field Company Australian Engineers. But even he died of wounds sustained during the Battle of the Somme.

For the third year in a row the festive season was a subdued affair in Frome. As the *Somerset & Wilts Journal* reported it:

Sergeant Albert Parsons, of the Somerset Light Infantry, was also killed on 1 July 1916 – the first day of The Somme. Like so many other soldiers who died that day, he has no known grave.

The village of Mells was home to the Horners who, along with many other families in the village, lost loved ones during the First World War.

Corporal George Hanney, of the Monmouthshire Regiment, was killed in action on 8 May 1915, aged 19. He would be the first of three brothers to lose their lives in the conflict.

Almost a month to the day after his brother George died, Private Frederick Hanney, of the Somerset Light Infantry, was also killed. Like his brother, he has no known grave.

Private Alexander Hanney became the third Hanney brother to be killed, when he died of wounds in May 1916. Like his two brothers, he is commemorated on the Frome War Memorial.

'Christmas has passed off surprisingly quiet in Frome. So far as one could judge, the terrible crowd of people who, according to the powers-that-be, were certain to rush off everywhere by train, calmly stayed at home. Everybody took their pleasures, or stifled their sorrows, quietly. Not even one roysterer imbibed so freely of the flowing bowl as to land him in the toils of the majesty of the law. The weather seems to have behaved itself fairly well, too, so that, taking everything into consideration, Christmas, 1916, might conceivably have been worse.'

For at least one Frome family, however, this Christmas was much worse than any previous one. The Hanneys, of 132 Marston Road, spent the festive period in mourning for their three eldest sons lost to the war. Corporal George Hanney, aged 19, of the 3rd Battalion Monmouthshire Regiment had been killed in action on 8 May 1915. A month later his brother, Frederick, aged 18, shared the same fate while serving as a private with 1/Somersets. And then on 26 May 1916, their younger brother, Private Alexander Hanney of the 5th Battalion Royal Berkshire Regiment succumbed to wounds he had sustained previously. Although the CWGC gives Alexander's age as 18, he was only 11 at the time of the 1911 Census, so therefore it means he was just 16 when he died.

If not openly spoken on the streets of Frome or elsewhere, then certainly the feeling must have existed in the minds of the local population, at the end of 1916, as to 'how much longer will this war continue?' Perhaps it was better that they did not know.

CHAPTER 6

Seeing it Through (Jan–Dec 1917)

In retrospect, 1917 is seen by historians as the 'year of disasters' for the Allied armies. These included the failure of the French Army's spring offensive and subsequent mutiny – along with the British one at Etaples – the Russian Revolution, leading ultimately to their withdrawal from the war, and the Third Battle of Ypres, also known as Passchendaele, which ranks along with The Somme in terms of human cost. But it wasn't all doom and gloom. There was a change of government in Britain to herald in the year, with David Lloyd George becoming the new Prime Minister, the entry of America into the war in April, and the advances in technology for the front lines, including tanks and aircraft. The seeds of victory that would finally be achieved the following year were sown in this one.

It was a year that would also see the people of Frome dig even deeper in their efforts to support the war, adopting voluntary rationing, engaging in acts of self-sacrifice, individually and collectively, and ensuring, through their continuous work in such organisations as the Frome Prisoner of War Fund, the message from back home was one of dogged determination. It was a message that had a much needed morale-boosting effect on those men on the front line or in prisoner-of-war camps. That is not to say there was no uncertainty in Frome, as with the war now entering its fourth year and no end to it in sight, along

"For Liberty!——the last, but not the least!"

America entered the war on the British side in April 1917, although their actual presence on the Western Front would not be felt for some time.

with the sheer number of families mourning loved ones, it was perhaps understandable if at times the people of the town and outlying areas felt down. The severe and biting cold that would be a companion of this winter did not help matters either. At times like these, then, the local population no doubt looked to the church for inspiration and

The service to inaugurate the War Shrine in St. John's Churchyard, March 1917.

continued faith and it seemed, in Frome at least, that whatever denomination you chose, your spiritual needs would be catered for.

Frome's somewhat chequered religious history had seen a tradition of orthodox and non-conformist groups co-existing in the town, however uncomfortable at times this may have been, stretching all the way back to the Reformation. The main split, however, came about when the monarchy was restored after the Civil War and a return to the Anglican tradition, from Protestantism, was ordered. John Humfry, vicar of St John's church, refused and in 1662 left the church, with many of his congregation, to worship up the road at Rook Lane.

By the time of the First World War there were all manner of churches, chapels, meeting-rooms, halls and private houses catering to the needs of groups such as Baptists, Quakers, Wesleyans, Christadelphians, Congregationalists, Anglicans, Methodists and even a chapter of the Plymouth Brethren.

As well as ministering to the spiritual needs of their congregations, several also commemorated those of their number that were fighting in the war, or had been killed doing so. One such war shrine was unveiled in March 1917 at St John's Church – where Humfry had been vicar all those years before. It was dedicated to those men serving in the armed forces, living or dead, who had a connection to the church. In a short address, the vicar, the Reverend W. Randolph – who in August 1914, at the outbreak of the war, had had the difficult journey back to Frome after being stranded in Switzerland – said other names would be added to the list 'as they came in and opportunity offered'. As well as a shrine to those in the war, it also stood there as a call to prayer and that he hoped a prayer would ascend from one of his congregation each time they passed by it.

> *'Let them remember in prayer all those heroes who went forth to roll back the tide of war from their very doors, and especially those who had made the supreme sacrifice.'*

Although the various congregations around the town had seen a depletion of numbers, through men being away fighting, this was off-set to some degree by the soldiers stationed in Frome who regularly attended church. These were men of the Royal Field Artillery who, at

A group of Royal Field Artillery recruits who came to Frome for training.

the start of 1917, had been based on and off in the town for more than three years.

Frome was used to the sight of khaki uniforms in and around the town, as the North Somerset Yeomanry had held their annual summer training camp the year before the war and, at the outbreak of it, the Royal Medical Corps, route-marching their way back from camp, stopped in the town for the purposes of mobilisation and stayed for more than a week. These experiences though, would be quite different to the Royal Field Artillery's stay, which turned Frome more or less into a garrison town.

The first contingent of soldiers, numbering around 300, had arrived in Frome on Monday, 23 November 1914. These were recruits to the 25th Division of the Royal Field Artillery. An advanced party had come to town on the previous Saturday to make certain everything was ready. This included the Market Hall – before its use as a munitions factory for J.W. Singer and Sons – where the men would initially be quartered. On alighting at Frome railway station, around 6.30am on the Monday, the mainly Glaswegian contingent, as reported by the *Somerset Standard*, made their presence known to the sleeping residents of Portway by singing out a rousing version of *It's A Long Way To Tipperary*. They then marched through the streets to the Market Hall, where they were joined the next day by a further 400 recruits. Eventually, the number of men stationed in Frome would reach almost 3,000.

After this initial period, the Royal Field Artillery moved onto a piece of open land in Frome, called the Leaze, opposite what is today called Mendip View. This was the spot the North Somerset Yeomanry had used for its training camp in 1913. Being on such elevated ground meant that any rainfall would easily drain away and so made an ideal location for a temporary army base.

The Artillery recruits would stay in Frome for the duration of their training – lasting around twelve weeks – before leaving for the front, their places then being taken by another batch of recruits. Once the full complement of troops had arrived in Frome, the War Office acquired as many vacant buildings, public and private, they could find to accommodate the officers and non-ranking men.

The 25th Division of the Royal Field Artillery coming through the Market Place on their way to Sunday service.

From the very beginning of the soldiers' stay the majority of local people did everything they could to make them feel part of the community. Various clubs, halls and rooms around town opened their doors, providing the troops with not only traditional pub games such as billiards and darts, but also daily papers and magazines, subsidised refreshments and several pianos. There was also space put aside for those who wanted to write letters home, a table and writing materials being provided, normally free of charge.

As mentioned earlier, the churches and chapels put on special services for the men, along with arranging entertainment in the form of concerts and plays. One such 'company' was the Portway United Methodist Church, who put on several productions.

Sporting events were arranged for the soldiers as well, including many football matches, which were usually either against different army units or local teams. An example of this took place on Boxing Day 1914. The Frome civilians won the encounter, according to the *Somerset Standard*, scoring three goals against the artillerymen, while keeping a clean sheet themselves. A later encounter, also reported in the newspaper, provided an even bigger score-line: that of five-nil to the civilians.

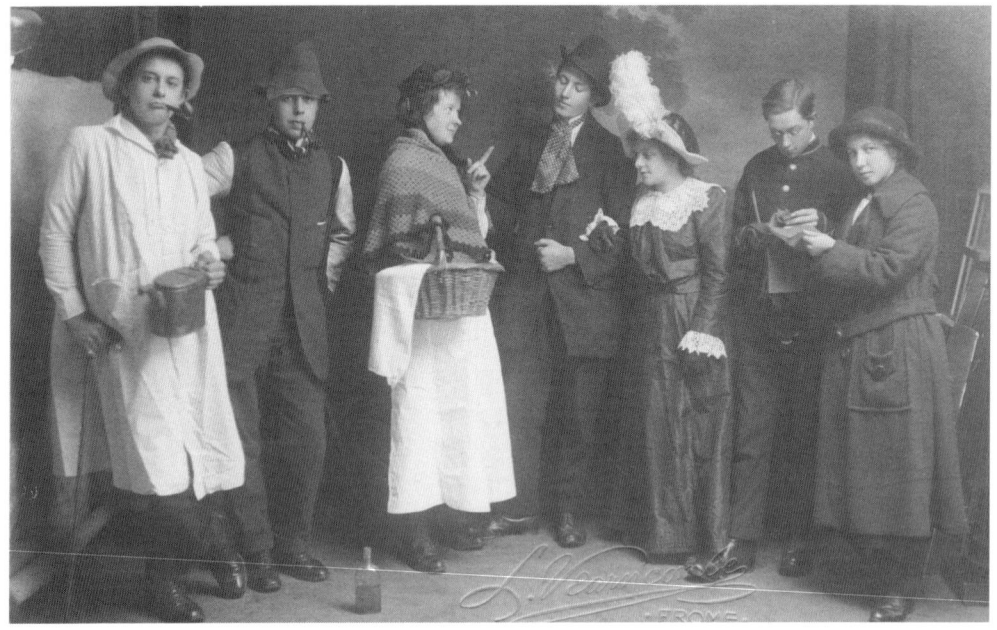

The 'Portway Players' provided entertainment for the stationed Royal Field Artillerymen.

The Victoria Jubilee Baths opened its doors to the artillerymen, but initially with restricted times. As more and more of them came into town and used the bathing facilities, however, it came to a point where they were given exclusive use of the baths (except for Thursdays between four in the afternoon to eight o'clock in the evening, which was given over for use by the women of the town).

Victoria Jubilee Swimming Baths.

Although each batch of recruits stayed in Frome for only twelve weeks, there was always sadness around their leaving, as many friendships with local people had developed. There was, of course, also the uncertainty about what the future held for them, as inevitably they would be sent overseas to one theatre of war or another, with this being, more likely than not, the Western Front. Many of the artillerymen who left Frome kept in contact, usually by letters or postcards. One person who did was Gunner Will Hyde. In one of his letters to a

Gunner Will Hyde, who undertook his training in Frome.

The first page of Will Hyde's letter, dated 29 April 1917.

group of friends he made while undertaking his training here, he wrote:

> '*I entered Frome, as a stranger in a strange country. I leave it,*
> *however, with regret, knowing that I have left behind friends to*
> *whom I am greatly indebted, for my happy hours I have spent*
> *there, during my short stay. I certainly cannot find words with*
> *which to express my heartfelt thanks, your kindness and*
> *generosity was greatly appreciated.*'

By 1917, No.7 Depot of the Royal Field Artillery was billeted here, to which Gunner Hyde belonged. They finally left Frome in the spring of that year, but not before they were involved in some extra-curricular activities, so to speak, as two incidents in the April required their assistance, outside normal duties.

The first episode the artillerymen were involved in was offering their military presence in what the *Somerset Standard* called '*the most sensational scene witnessed in Frome for a number of years*'. The incident involved a local resident called Captain Ryall, who lived at Critchill Lodge, about a mile from the town centre. Under long-term medical care for recurring problems with his brain, which would often lead to violent outbursts, he was now thought to have temporarily recovered. He had a military background, having served among others with the Lancashire Fusiliers, was a talented scholar and also a barrister-at-law. On

A poem written by three Artillerymen who had been stationed in Frome during their training.

R. F. A.
(Require Fresh Attractions)

Three lovesick soldier lads are we,
Willie, Freddie and Ber-tie;
We loved three damsels don't you see,
Jennie, Lily and Lu-cy.

Since we left our humble home,
Since we came down here to Frome,
Lily, Lucy and Jen-nie,
Have jilted us poor mortals three.

But he who must be pitied most,
Is poor old Bert, almost a ghost;
His sleep disturbed, his mind uneasy,
He can't stop thinking of his Lucy.

Poor William's hurt, no doubt of that,
Her gifts he treasures still, alack!
But, Lily, she must be a mug,
To tread like that on poor old Spud.

And then there's Fred, poor fellow, he
Had thought his true love was Jennie;
But now that love has turned to hate,
Advise him to look after Kate.

So when we get into the trench,
When we each think of our wench;
We shall dash into the fray,
And just for spite we'll wound and slay.

So Jennie, Lily, Lucy dears,
Remember we've one thing that cheers;
French girls we'll cuddle and we'll hug,
So good-bye from each poor Frome mug.

Saturday, 21 April 1917, however, he began to experience another 'attack' and his doctor was called.

At first, the physician, Doctor Rattray, was able to calm him and then left. When returning to the house in the early hours the following morning, after being called out again, Captain Ryall attacked the doctor with a sword. As the flat of the 2-inch, double-edged blade came towards his head, Rattray moved out of the way, but was hit on the shoulder, badly bruising it. The doctor tried to make his escape down the driveway but the captain also had a rifle and began firing at him. By the time the police were summoned, the captain was ensconced in his house, taking pot shots at anything or anyone that moved. It was then the men from the Royal Field Artillery were called out.

After marching from their barracks to the house they surrounded it and a gun battle ensued, watched by an ever-increasing crowd of onlookers from the authorities and the public alike. Eventually, as the artillerymen closed in, Captain Ryall broke cover and was felled by two shots, one from a rifle that penetrated his thigh and a revolver shot which entered one side of his face, traversed his jaw, and then exited the other. Once firmly secured, Captain Ryall was taken to Victoria Hospital, where his injuries were treated, and then to Shepton Mallet prison, in order to stand trial. A tragic postscript to this story is that a few months later, while still in prison, he committed suicide.

The second occasion soldiers from the Royal Field Artillery undertook a role outside their normal duties, was to act as guard of honour at a funeral. Private Everett Ferriday was just 18 years old and had only recently enlisted in the 94th Territorial Reserve Battalion of the Gloucestershire Regiment when he died from bronchial pneumonia after catching a chill. Although born in Cornwall and living elsewhere before signing up, he had several 'happy' connections to Frome, according to his friends, and so it was decided to bury him in the town. He was to be given a military funeral and, after his body was received by the Royal Field Artillery on its arrival in Frome, his coffin was conveyed through the town on a gun carriage, draped with a Union Jack. Hundreds of people lined the streets to watch the procession to Vallis Road Cemetery, where artillerymen fired three volleys over the grave and the 'Last Post' was sounded by the battery bugler.

The Victoria Hospital where Captain Ryall was taken after he was 'captured'.

After the bulk of artillerymen had departed Frome, commander of No.7 Depot, Colonel H.W. Addington, wrote to Mr Woodland, the chairman of Frome Urban District Council:

'to express to you, and through you to the inhabitants of the town, our appreciation of the kindness, consideration and hospitality extended to all ranks of the depot during its stay in Frome, and for the cordial co-operation of the urban authorities on the occasions we have had to seek their assistance. It is extremely gratifying for me to reflect on the good feeling existing between the civil population and the military. We leave you with regret and cordial farewells.'

The gravestone in Vallis Road cemetery of Everett Ferriday.

As we have seen, a part of this hospitality given by the Frome people to the Royal Field Artillery was through the provision of entertainment, which played a major role in keeping up the spirits and morale of the

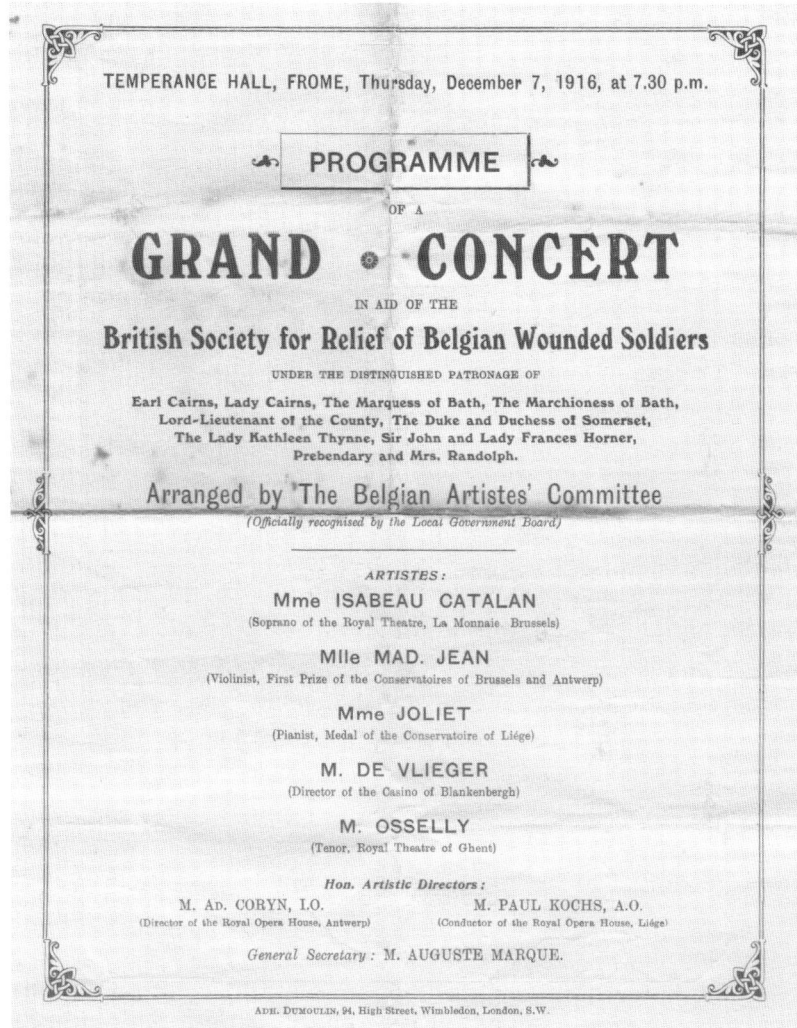

TEMPERANCE HALL, FROME, Thursday, December 7, 1916, at 7.30 p.m.

PROGRAMME

OF A

GRAND ❀ CONCERT

IN AID OF THE

British Society for Relief of Belgian Wounded Soldiers

UNDER THE DISTINGUISHED PATRONAGE OF

Earl Cairns, Lady Cairns, The Marquess of Bath, The Marchioness of Bath,
Lord-Lieutenant of the County, The Duke and Duchess of Somerset,
The Lady Kathleen Thynne, Sir John and Lady Frances Horner,
Prebendary and Mrs. Randolph.

Arranged by The Belgian Artistes' Committee

(*Officially recognised by the Local Government Board*)

ARTISTES :

Mme ISABEAU CATALAN
(Soprano of the Royal Theatre, La Monnaie Brussels)

Mlle MAD. JEAN
(Violinist, First Prize of the Conservatoires of Brussels and Antwerp)

Mme JOLIET
(Pianist, Medal of the Conservatoire of Liége)

M. DE VLIEGER
(Director of the Casino of Blankenbergh)

M. OSSELLY
(Tenor, Royal Theatre of Ghent)

Hon. Artistic Directors :

M. AD. CORYN, I.O.   M. PAUL KOCHS, A.O.
(Director of the Royal Opera House, Antwerp)   (Conductor of the Royal Opera House, Liége)

General Secretary : M. AUGUSTE MARQUE.

ADH. DUMOULIN, 94, High Street, Wimbledon, London, S.W.

The front sheet of the Belgian Concert concert programme, which took place in December 1916.

men. But it wasn't just those in khaki stationed in the town that benefited. A few months earlier, in December 1916, a Grand Concert had been put on at the Temperance Hall in Frome to aid the British Society for Relief of Belgian Wounded Soldiers. The poster for the event announced it had been arranged by 'The Belgian Artistes' committee, and the programme consisted of a mixture of operatic excerpts from the likes of *La Bohème* and *Tosca*, along with instrumental soloists playing works by composers such as Grieg, Debussy and Franck. The connection with Belgium, of course, went back to the outset of the war in 1914 when fifty Belgian refugees, fleeing the advancing German army in their country, had been given sanctuary in Frome. Also, the first patients admitted to the Relief Hospital at Longleat had been wounded Belgian soldiers. It was also a demonstration of how integrated the refugees had become in their new community that by the time of this concert all were employed in or around the town.

In any war, either back home or on the front line, entertainment plays a key role in keeping up morale and allowing respite from the horrors and hardship, if only for the duration of a play, concert or even a song. For most of Frome people providing entertainment it was quite localised, such as the aforementioned Portway Methodist Church Players, with their productions for the Royal Field Artillerymen. For one Frome man, however, involvement was on a national level and entertaining the troops, more often than not, meant those in the front line. This man was Robert Stannard, who before the war had been the organist at St John's Church in Frome (and no doubt had his name on the war shrine). He had joined the Royal Fusiliers in January 1915, aged 17, and had already seen action at Gallipoli and in France, before being 'talent spotted' in early 1917 and asked to help form a divisional concert party (he belonged to the 29th Infantry Division). The ensemble of performers put together – he himself taking the role of accompanist – became one of the most well-known and famous of all concert parties: The Diamond Troupe. They were so named after the divisional sign of a red triangle worn on each shoulder, which, when joined together, formed a diamond.

Once auditions took place and performers selected – from sixty hopefuls, eight were chosen – it was decided the show would run in two parts. The first half was to be based on Pierrot, the famous stock character of *commedia dell'arte* and music hall, while the second half was to be variety, including a trick cyclist, vocalist and a female

The famous Diamond Troupe. Robert Stannard is seated third from left in centre row.

impersonator known as 'Queenie'. Apparently the soldier 'playing' her was so good, he fooled many of the audience.

The Diamond Troupe had been formed in Arras, where the 29th Division's headquarters were based at that time. Once the company was ready to perform, however, they played concerts throughout the Western Front, delivering perhaps up to six performances in a month. They also gave a number of concerts back in England, one being at the Royal Court Theatre, watched by Queen Alexandra, the Queen Mother, and entitled: 'A Show From the Trenches'.

It wasn't just men such as Robert Stannard that had specific skills to offer in supporting soldiers through non-combatant roles. Many women did too. One such woman was Mary Frances Symes-Bullen, a Volunteer Aid Detachment nurse. Mary, the daughter of Colonel John Bullen Symes-Bullen JP, lived in Charmouth, Devon and was a trained physiotherapist and masseuse. In the summer of 1915 she offered her services to Lady Bath at the Military Relief Hospital at Longleat.

Between the arrival of the initial patients – Belgian soldiers – in November 1914 and that of Mary, or 'Nurse' Bullen, as she became known at Longleat, the hospital had gone through several changes. The first 'British' soldiers were admitted in January 1915 (in fact they were

Envelope addressed to Mary 'Nurse' Bullen.

Lady Bath's letter in reply to Nurse Bullen's offer of assistance.

all Indian troops who had been billeted at Winchester for the winter, the change of climate causing many to become sick) and these were followed by an intake from Alexandra Hospital, Cosham. In this latter batch of patients were two members of the original British Expeditionary Force. After the majority of these patients had been treated and discharged, many of the beds lay empty, because the size of the hospital was not large enough to persuade the Ambulance Train to stop at Warminster. Accordingly, it was decided to install an operating theatre in what was Lady Kathleen's bedroom and expand the number of beds to fifty-five and then later, when this did not entice additional patients, to further increase it to ninety.

With the hospital now full of convalescing soldiers whose wounded limbs required all manner of nursing care, massage and 'electrical treatment', Nurse Bullen's expertise greatly benefited the hospital and its patients. Although she was trained as a physiotherapist and masseuse there seems to be no record of her having undertaken any formal training as a nurse, but during her time at Longleat she was informally

'Nurse' Bullen outside Longleat House with several of its military residents.

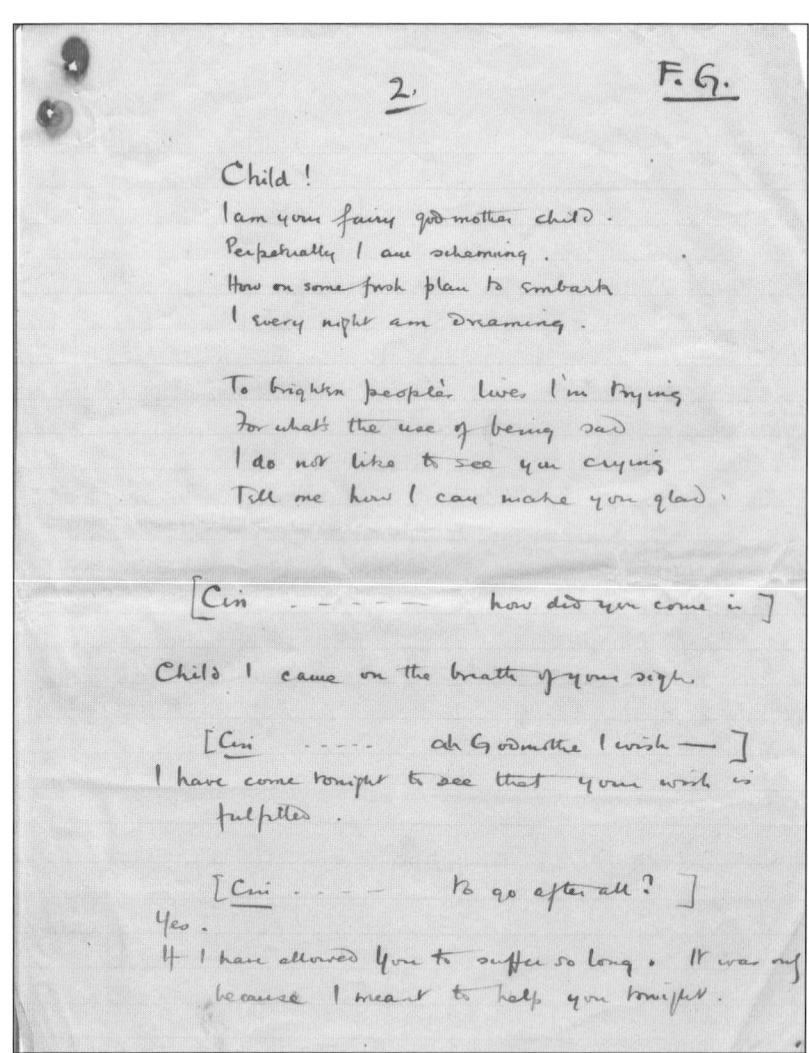

A page of the Christmas Pantomime script in which Nurse Bullen played the Fairy Godmother.

given the title of 'nurse' and later 'sister'. As well as her role as a VAD nurse, she became involved in the activities the staff organised, including plays and sketches. In one such outing she played the 'Fairy Godmother', while in another she is recorded as a 'Little Girl'.

In January 1917, in that month's *Longleat Lyre,* it was announced that:

'Miss Bullen, our V.A.D. Masseuse, has left us to take a short holiday before she takes up work in the South of France. Miss Bullen has been a very hard worker here for nearly two years, and we are all extremely sorry to lose her, but we hope that after her term of work in France she will return to us.'

Mary Bullen did return to work at Longleat, in November 1917, but during her time in France had been honourably mentioned in despatches. After the war, she married Lieutenant Colonel Sir Philip Colfox, a Baronet and later Conservative MP. They had four children. She died in 1973.

In May 1917, while Nurse Bullen was in France, Longleat and the neighbouring areas, including Frome, experienced a bout of severe weather. As the newspaper reported it:

'About quarter to nine on the evening of last Saturday [12 May] *a most violent storm, such as had not occurred for a great many years, took place in this district. The rain came down in sheets, and was followed by heavy thunder and lightning.... . In the lower portions of the town, notably in the Market Place and King Street, there were early symptoms of flooding.'*

In the course of the storm a resident was struck by lightning, according to the report. Mrs Strent, of Butts Hill, had her baby in her arms when the discharge from a bolt of lightening knocked them to the ground, leaving her bruised and shaken but thankfully her child unhurt. And in the aftermath of the rains, and reminiscent of December 1914, several places in the town centre became completely flooded.

If water caused damage for certain buildings during May, then fire completely gutted another in October. That building was Park House, owned by the Horner family of Mells. The fire began in heating equipment installed in a recently-built wing by a former tenant and before it could be brought under control had gutted the interior of the ancient mansion.

The Horner family had procured the Manor of Mells from the Crown in 1543 – and not through the chance discovery in a deed-filled

King Street, Frome. Flood water is beginning to recede.

The same street a hundred years later.

pie, as the nursery-rhyme about Little Jack Horner would have us believe. In the early eighteenth century a descendant abandoned the residential Manor House and moved into the newly-built Mells Park House. Here the Horners remained until 1900 when, finding it too expensive to continue living there, Sir John and Lady Horner moved back to the Manor House and let out Park House.

Further tragedy would befall the Horner family the following month with the death of Edward Horner. Having gone through the grief of losing their son-in-law – Raymond Asquith, son of the then Prime

THE FIRE AT MELLS PARK.

HISTORIC MANSION DESTROYED.

SPLENDID AND HEROIC SALVAGE WORK BY MEN AND WOMEN.

FIRE FOUGHT TO THE LAST.

THE MANSION BEFORE THE FIRE.

As narrated briefly in our issue of Friday last in the first and second editions and more fully in the third edition, a disastrous fire occurred during Thursday night which completely destroyed the noble residence of Sir John F. F. Horner. The fire broke out in a comparatively new heating apparatus which the late tenant put in, Sir J. F. F. Horner informs us with his full approval, to warm the house with hot water instead of hot air as it used to be. It was the stove or its connections which heated the hot water which started the fire in a recently-built wing added by the late Mr. Gilbert Bates. The first intimation that anything was amiss occurred just before 7 o'clock. There were only two housemaids in the house at the time. They first noticed the smoke about, but by the time they got to the stove, about 7 p.m., the little room in the basement where it stood was all in a blaze. The housemaids behaved extraordinarily well and pluckily, but soon found there was nothing to do but to give the alarm, which was promptly attended to by all who became aware of it.

A telephone message was dispatched to the Police Station at Frome, the hooter was sounded about 8 o'clock, and the Fire Brigade were summoned, but no horses or other means of traction were available, although application was made in all directions for over an hour. A couple of horses were at last obtained for the steamer.

The alarm was also given in the village and vicinity, and ready helpers soon mustered. Sir John Horner and his daughters were in the neighbourhood at the Manor House, where they usually reside when at Mells, but Lady Horner was in London.

The newspaper report of the Mells Manor House fire.

Minister – the previous year, they now lost their only surviving son. Lieutenant Edward Horner had only recently been back with his family at Mells on leave before he died. According to *The Times* obituary, as reported in the *Somerset Standard,* Lieutenant Horner first held a commission in the North Somerset Yeomanry before transferring to the 18th (Queen Mary's Own) Hussars. He went to France in February 1915, but was wounded three months later, so seriously, in fact, it was thought he would never be able to fight again. After a dangerous, but successful operation, followed by a long period of convalescence, Edward did recover and was sent on light duty to Egypt around a year after he had originally arrived in France. Eventually passed fully fit for active service once more, he rejoined the Hussars in March 1917, fighting on the Western Front. On 21 November, however, at Noyelles on the Somme he was killed in action from a gunshot wound to the chest.

Another notable local death happened in the final month of the year. Whereas the Manor of Mells was in the hands of the Horner family, that of Frome belonged to the Duckworths. Head of the family for the past forty years had been the Reverend William Arthur Duckworth. His contribution to the community of Frome and the surrounding area, during the four decades he presided over the manor, was beyond reproach. He died on Thursday, 6 December 1917, with the following week's *Somerset Standard* reporting that:

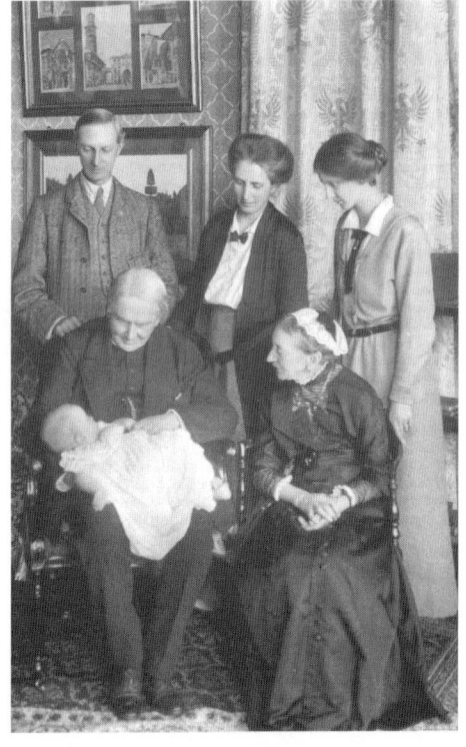

'*It was everywhere locally on Friday last a subject of comment, with deep regret, that one of the most valued men of the district had passed to rest.*'

The Reverend Arthur Duckworth with his great grandchild, and other members of his family, pictured the year before he died.

Like Robert Stannard of the Diamond Troupe, another man with connections to Frome and whose particular skills had been recognised by the armed forces was George Bradbury. Born in Shepton Mallet, he had been a keen and clever amateur photographer during his school days and decided to make it his profession on finishing his education. He went to work for Bell & Sons of Frome and Shepton Mallet. George worked in the Frome branch, located in Catherine Street, at the top of the long cobbled thoroughfare ascending south-west from the centre. He obviously took to the job well, as he eventually took over running the branch until the war came along and he joined the Somerset Regiment. Once his skill as a photographer was recognised, he became an air mechanic with 6 Squadron Royal Flying Corps.

Before the war George Bradbury had successfully run the photographic business of Bell & Sons on Catherine Street in Frome.

The Royal Flying Corps was a fairly new addition to the British armed forces. It had originally existed as an army unit, initially as a Balloon Section and then as the Air Battalion of the Royal Engineers. At the same time, the Royal Navy had its own section, namely the Royal Naval Air Service. To start with, the new corps had a reputation for recruiting those who regarded flying more as a hobby and, perhaps not surprisingly, most of the pilots and observers came from upper-class families (especially those who had access to aircraft pre-war). The engineers, on the other hand, were mainly skilled workmen in their

Although a dangerous occupation, the value of aerial photography was quickly realised.

civilians lives, who had either been employed maintaining vehicles or had a trade such as map-making or photography to their name.

Balloon observation, the forerunner to aerial photography, was a dangerous undertaking, as once in the basket suspended under a balloon and winched to a suitable height, the observers became easy targets. Aircraft eventually took over this role and it was thought at one time that they should only be used for observation and reconnaissance. As the combative side of this new air force increased, so did that of information gathering. Photographs of enemy territory could be closely examined on the ground (by generals miles behind the front lines, no doubt!) so the development of aerial reconnaissance came into its own. This is where George Bradbury shone. Once airborne, it was far from easy to take aerial photographs; the large cameras were difficult to handle, not helped by the fact they were located outside the aircraft. The occupants would also be recipients of intense enemy fire, either from the ground or from other aircraft. And once photographs had been taken, developing them could be just as hard.

During the First World War aerodromes were usually nothing more than a field or two with living accommodation and maintenance buildings located near by. At the airfield George Bradbury was stationed, he set up his studio in one of these buildings. From his diary it seems the aerodrome had been singled out for special attention from the German Air Force in the weeks leading up to the end of October. In the early hours of the 31st the airfield once more came under attack and by all accounts a direct hit on the studio, where George was working, killed him instantly.

Five days before his death he wrote to his brother. In the letter he said:

'Dear Bert. I was awfully pleased to hear from you today and such a jolly long letter too. I heard of the fire at Mells Park as it was in the daily papers, which we get out here and Peg told me of it too. Do the air raids put the wind up you much? Glad you were not too near and no one was hurt. I expect I have been nearer than you to the noisy toads but it is wonderful how little damage they do for such nasty contrivances. We get used to even them in time. It is wonderful what one can get used to isn't it. No need to tell them this at home though. Do you ever see Fritz in the searchlights; I have umpteen times at different times at different places and have seen several brought down. It is a sight worth seeing. I think our people have Fritz pretty well fixed in the air in spite of what one reads in the papers … . I see that you sometimes meet fellows from places near home. I have met several out here too. No more now so I will close with love. Yours as ever, George.'

George Bradbury was just one of the many men with connections to Frome who died in 1917. On 2 April that year, the day before 18-year-old new recruit Everett Ferriday had succumbed to bronchial pneumonia, the highest-ranking and oldest soldier linked to the town died. Brigadier General Francis John De Gex CB CMG of the General Staff had been born in Frome in the early 1860s, the son of the Reverend F. De Gex. Educated at Oxford University and the military academy at Sandhurst, he was the Base Commandant at Rouen, formerly of the Duke of Wellington's (West Riding Regiment). He was 55 years old when he died.

In June, the *Somerset Standard* reported news of three Frome men killed in the same action. They were Albert Sherstone (23), Ralph Butt (24) and Arthur Bailey (22). All were riflemen with the 20th Battalion King's Royal Rifle Corps. The men were engaged in consolidating work on a position they had only recently taken from the Germans, when there was a heavy counter-attack. During the bombardment a shell exploded where the men were working and killed them instantly. Seven other men from Frome were injured throughout this enemy barrage. According to David L. Adams, in his book *Frome's Fallen Heroes: The Great War*, Lance Corporal Bailey was actually from Croscombe in Somerset, not Frome, as reported in the *Standard*. Also, Rifleman Butt is listed as being killed on 19 June 1917, whereas the other two are recorded as 17 June. The discrepancy may come from the fact that he was originally listed as missing in action, but possibly it was a mistake at some point in the official process of recording the death.

Later in the year, during the Third Battle of Ypres, four more local men died on the same day, 4 October, each one from a different regiment: Private Fred Barnes of 1/Somersets; Private Robert Gamble of 8/Devonshires; Lance Corporal Stanley Heyluer of 1/Duke of Cornwall's; and Private William Snell of 5/Dorsetshire. All the men lived in Frome, except Lance Corporal Heyluer who lived nearby in Beckington; all have no known graves and are commemorated on the Tyne Cot Memorial, at Zonnebeke, in Belgium.

Two days after Christmas Day 1917, Corporal Walter Yeoman was discharged from the army due to ill health. He had enlisted in 1915, joining the Mechanical Transport Section of the Army Service Corps and saw action in France, before being sent back home suffering from rheumatism. Several years before the war he had been a distinguished cyclist and world record holder.

Walter Shepherd Yeoman was born at 3 Christchurch Street West, Frome, in 1876 and developed a keen interest in cycling. He joined the Silverdale Cycle Club around the age of 16 and within a couple of years had broken several of the club's records. His greatest achievement though came in July 1895. Riding a tandem with a partner, J.B. Cooke, he covered one hundred miles in 3hrs 47mins and 21secs, setting a new world record that stood for the next nine years. Subsequently, he rode in numerous professional races, winning many of them, until he retired from cycling in 1898.

The devastating effect that war had on sport and its participants is perhaps one of the great untold tragedies. Although Walter Yeoman had finished his sporting activities by the time the war started, many other Frome men would be cut down in their prime, either through war injuries that prevented them

Walter Yeoman.

taking part in their chosen sport again or else they had been killed. The list of those killed in action included well-known local footballers such as Bert Dix, Charlie Thompson, Charlie White, Fred Clarke, Brinsley

Frome Town AFC pictured before the war. Many of its players, along with other local sportsmen, would serve King and Country but not return.

Palmer, Reg Moody and Albert Jolliffe, rugby players including Harold Biggs, Frank Andrews and Charles Young, and cricketers such as Edward Burr, William Curwen and Alan Ross; along with a whole host of others in sports as diverse as hockey, boxing, water polo, sword fighting and athletics.

Whether Able Seaman Noad from Rode, just outside Frome, played sports or possessed any special skills is unknown, at least to the author of this book, but he is included in, and brings to a close, this particular chapter due to the date of his death. He was killed in action on Monday, 31 December, and so became the last serviceman from the Frome area to die in 1917.

CHAPTER 7

The Final Blows
(Jan 1918 onwards)

Although the people of Frome did not know it yet, as the bells prepared to chime midnight at end of 1917, the New Year of 1918 would be the last under the cloud of conflict (at least for the next twenty years or so). The position of the war was still a stalemate, but each side knew they would have to make a decisive offensive in the coming months. The British and German armies faced acute manpower shortages and those who had been conscripted did not always possess the same fighting spirit as those before them. But whereas the attacks on British supply lines had not managed to starve its people into submission, the

Christmas and New Year cards would not be sent in war time again for at least twenty years.

blockade of Germany was complete and with the bad winter the previous year, a severe shortage of crops merely added to the people's suffering.

The British also had the Americans on their side, with their ally bringing men, munitions and materials into France and ultimately this would prove to be a deciding factor. The Germans, realising it was 'now or never', undertook one last great offensive in the spring of 1918. Employing the new tactic of using small groups of elite shock troops to spearhead attacks, the Germans managed to breach British lines in several places, in March 1918, causing huge casualties. Due to their over-extended supply lines and exhaustion of Germany's other troops though, the offensive ran out of steam and they were forced to withdraw. The following month they tried again but due to the spirit of the British resistance, this offensive was called off as well.

Prior to this encounter, the British Army's Commander-in-Chief, Sir Douglas Haig, had issued an 'Order of the Day' which stated, in no uncertain terms, and echoed Nelson's famous signal before the Battle of Trafalgar, exactly what was required of each man:

> *'There is no other course open to us but to fight it out! Every position must be held to the last man; there must be no retirement. With our backs to the wall and believing in the justice of our cause, each one of us must fight on to the end.'*

Once the fighting began, the men adhered to the order to the letter.

The years between 1914 and 1918 saw disruption to the schools in Frome, but this was not always due to the war. Outbreaks of disease did as much to close schools and disrupt the educational process as the events going on across the Channel and elsewhere in the world. The influenza epidemic of 1918 obviously had a devastating effect on educational establishments, but other, mainly childhood diseases, made their presence known long before.

According to its record books, the Infants department at the Milk Street School was closed for a week after the summer holiday in 1914, due to whooping cough. An outbreak of the same disease affected the Wesley School two years later. It closed its doors on 25 January 1916 and did not open again properly until early March. They did attempt to reopen in February, but only ten children were in attendance. Even when they finally reopened on 6 March, there were only four more children present.

Diphtheria also caused serious disruption during the war years. In July 1917 Wesley Girls School closed for a month and then again in September, when the mistress reported that 'Owing to the school having been closed… on account of cases of diphtheria, many parents have become scared and have removed their children from the school.' In this report, she also lists the names of girls whose parents had now taken their children somewhere else. Eleven of them had gone to Milk Street, one to Christ Church and one to St John's.

Wesley Boys was not immune to the outbreak either, or to parents removing their children, especially after a boy died of the disease there in September 1917. According to Derek Gill, in his book *School Days in Frome*: *'The County Medical Officer advised that all apparatus which children might put in their mouths be disinfected daily as a safeguard against another attack.'*

The following year it was the turn of Christ Church School to suffer an outbreak. Phyllis Marne was discovered to have diphtheria on 21 February 1918, although it was another girl, Barbara White, who tragically died from it on St David's Day. Swabs continued to be taken constantly throughout the rest of the month and anyone found to have an inflamed throat was told to stay at home. Although there were no more deaths at the school, parents were obviously very concerned and attendance plummeted. The Easter holiday, on the advice of the doctor, was prolonged and the necessary fumigation and disinfection undertaken. At the end of April 1918 the school reopened, at which time the outbreak seemed to have abated.

Although it can be seen that disease was very disruptive, that is not to say the war did not have any impact on schools. As more and more male teachers were called up or enlisted, so the strain increased on the schools; this was especially true when news of former teachers being killed reached staff rooms and classrooms. One example, in 1918, was a teacher previously of the National School, located at the top of Bath Street.

'I have been informed that one of our assistant masters, Mr.
Edward Bruce Salmon, of the Gloucester Regiment, was killed
in the recent battle. He was called to the colours in April 1916.
He was in the trenches within three months of joining and saw
much active service afterwards. He was 25 years of age. He was
a young teacher of much promise and I feel his loss most deeply.'

The loss of any male relatives, be it their father, grandfather, uncle, brother or cousin, also had an adverse effect on the children and their education.

Due to the death of Edward Salmon, another member of staff, a Mr Pook, volunteered in April 1918. Even though he had been exempted from Army Service, he did so *'in view of the urgent call for men to resist the new great German offensive in Flanders'*. His place was taken at the school by a former pupil, who had been a first year student from college at the outbreak of war, had joined the army but was now temporarily released because of wounds.

At Vallis First School, in Milk Street, male teachers who left to fight were increasingly being replaced by female teachers who were, according to the log books of the time, 'less experienced'. The last male teacher left on 9 March 1917 and later that month it was recorded: *'Examined Standard V. This class is not getting on very well. The teacher is too young and has not power with* [the] *class, but there seems to be no help for it, as no* [other] *teachers are available.'*

It wasn't just lack of experience on the part of certain female teachers which caused problems. When their husbands or fiancés were home on leave, or else preparing to leave for the front, the teachers would, understandably, request leave. This would often cause conflict between teacher and school. One example occurred in October 1917. The husband of a teacher had ten days leave and so she asked for the same amount of time off. She was offered five days but in the end took the full amount anyway. On her return, she was asked to resign. What we may think of the school's action in today's perspective though, needs to be viewed in context. As Derek Gill writes: *'It seems a heartless action, but school life was very much affected by staff absences, causing disruption to the children's education.'*

Although the problem of relatively inexperienced female teachers replacing male counterparts did not affect Christ Church School, as they had no male teachers to begin with, nevertheless many of the female teachers still had similar needs at certain times, in regard to leave.

The lack of male teachers at certain schools and the increasing pressure of the war effort had the undue effect of pushing many children prematurely into work. As Mr Glover, Headmaster of the National School, wrote in February 1916: *'The senior boys are leaving school rapidly. The demand for labour is causing the parents to withdraw almost every boy as he reaches thirteen. Formerly a large number remained to* [fourteen].'

Elsewhere it was a similar story. At the British School it was noted senior boys were 'enticed' away from school the moment they could leave and, in some cases *'the last two months of a boy's school life are not spent at school at all.'*

Where the children were too young to leave for work, their contribution to the war effort was no less required. Throughout the war these boys and girls undertook many activities, from collecting everything from eggs and horse chestnuts to knitting socks for wounded soldiers. At the National School pupils also began to collect items for the parcels to be sent, via the Frome Prisoner of War Fund, to those local men who had been captured by the enemy. The boys' reward, other than knowing they were supporting the war effort, was to receive postcards from very grateful PoWs. One letter, from a Private Watts said: *'Thank you for your kindness towards us while being a prisoner in Germany, it tells us plainly that we are not forgotten at home.'*

At Christ Church School, from March 1915, the girls were encouraged to collect eggs for the wounded soldiers at the Red Cross Hospital in Keyford and within a few months had sent 1,200. Again, several of the recipients sent letters to the girls, expressing their gratitude. As well as eggs, the hospital's log books show that over the course of the war, the girls also collected and sent potatoes, marrows, beans, apples, plums, jam, parsnips, onions, beetroots, nuts and pears, as well as horse chestnuts (conkers). These, though the girls did not

Christ Church School: the class of 1915.

know it, were for use in manufacturing acetone for munitions. The pupils at the British School also collected conkers. In September 1917 80lbs were sent off, while in the following week 2cwt. By October 1917 the boys had collected a total of 14cwt.

As well as all this effort on the part of schools, circumstances were conspiring elsewhere against the Germans. During the summer and autumn things became worse for them; with their own allies either defeated or surrendered. The Italians forced the Austrians into retreat, ultimately resulting in the Austro-Hungarian government's request for peace. Meanwhile, the Serbs, along with British and French troops, moved against the Bulgarians and, once more, after a decisive victory (this time at the Battle of Vardar) their government capitulated and similarly requested peace. With Allied troops from the Balkans free to join the offensive against the Turks, an armistice with the Turks was agreed at the end of October.

This final blow of Turkey being out of the war left Germany alone and within two weeks, in November 1918, it too opened negotiations for an Armistice. On the eleventh day of that month, Germany finally agreed to the terms outlined in the agreement and signed it, with the Armistice coming into effect later that day, at 11am precisely. The news flashed around the world and was the trigger for celebrations in allied countries everywhere.

The end of the war, however, did not bring an end to Frome men dying. Many from the local areas died from wounds sustained while the conflict still raged, or else from various diseases. The deadliest of these was the Spanish flu – or influenza – pandemic which swept the globe in 1918 and the following year, estimated to have killed between three and six per cent of the world's population – more than all those killed in the First World War or the four years of the Black Death – and inflicting misery, pain and suffering on countless millions more.

Spanish flu made its lethal presence known in Frome during October 1918. Due to the number of pupils who had by then contracted it, schools closed their doors and were officially shut for five weeks. According to the records of Milk Street Girls School, influenza broke out in the town on 21 October 1918. Fifty-seven girls were absent that morning, rising to sixty-one in the afternoon. When the following morning eighty-one children failed to appear, the school closed.

Employers within the town fared no better, as they saw their workforces brutally depleted; Butler & Tanner reported 110 cases, J.W. Singer & Sons, 160 and as much as seventy per cent of Cockey's employees were off work through having the virus.

As the soldiers returned home after the Armistice, many of them arrived back in Frome already infected by the flu virus. One of these was Corporal Cyril Allen, of Keyford Terrace, who had served in the 3rd Battalion Royal Welsh Fusiliers.

Many other soldiers died from the flu while still abroad. These included 20-year-old Driver Frederick Gibson of the Royal Engineers who died on 23 October 1918 in Salonika and Private Ernest Young, aged 40, of the Mechanical Transport Company of the Army Service Corps, who died on 30 December 1918 in Greece. Deaths in France included the Reverend Harold Wood, aged 31, serving with the Royal Army Chaplains Department, and Ernest

Frederick Gibson was born in Frome and was 22 years old when he died. He is buried at the Doiran Military Cemetery, in Greece and his name appears on the Frome War Memorial.

Leach, aged 25, a Sergeant with the Royal Army Medical Corps who died on 9 February 1919 and is buried in the communal cemetery at St Germain-au-Mont-d'Or, near Lyon. Three months later, his father, Sergeant Albert Leach was able to visit his grave.

Ernest Leach died on 9 February 1918 of double pneumonia following influenza. He was just one of many Frome men who succumbed to the disease while still abroad after the war.

Sergeant Albert Leach stands at his son's graveside.

Despite the almost overwhelming number of victims worldwide, individual cases could still tug at heart strings. Eight-year-old Albert Goddard, for example, died in November 1918, while his father, Private Jesse Goddard, was still abroad in the trenches. Tragically, or perhaps disgustingly, Private Goddard only learnt of his son's death when he received the bill for the death certificate.

Frederick White, Frome postmaster, saw his oldest son die of influenza (while his youngest had died from wounds earlier in the war). Not long after his eldest son's death he wrote a letter to the mother of another victim, no doubt trying to provide comfort in her time of need, in which he said:

> *'I have felt very grieved for you too in your hour of great trial…*
> *My comfort is the result achieved by our boys. Our sacrifice is*
> *great but only think of the result. What it is. What it might have*
> *been had it not been for the grit of the lads. I hope dear madam*
> *that time will bring comfort to you also. The consciousness of*
> *your own splendid work for your country should help you.'*

The recipient of the letter was Mrs Milne-Redhead, whose daughter had died from complications arising from influenza, while the 'splendid work for your country' mentioned in the letter, referred to a local organisation she was involved in.

Throughout the First World War there had been various groups within Frome 'doing their bit' for the war effort, whether it was the Frome fanciers collecting eggs, the volunteers at the War Hospital supply depot, or the National Herb Association. The organisation Mrs Milne-Redhead was involved with, and indeed had started, became known as the Frome Prisoners of War Fund.

When Mrs Milne-Redhead began to read in the newspaper the names of local men who were being held in prisoner of war camps, and the terrible conditions under which they were believed to be held, she determined to do something to help. From her home in Trudoxhill, near Frome, she began to send parcels of food to the seven men she had heard about. Having begun as a private undertaking, it quickly became a more organised affair and was so successful that at the war's end no less than eighty-four prisoners had received parcels from the organisation at some time during the war. After the war, an official report on the fund was written. A copy was deposited with the Imperial War Museum in London, and it was also published in the *Somerset Standard* in April 1919.

[The Frome Prisoner of War Fund] *'was the first local fund to start, it is believed, in England on March 5th 1915. Countess Cairns, Mrs. Milne-Redhead and Mrs. Harold Smith met to discuss possible help for local prisoners of war in Germany about that date, and decided to start a fund to send food to the prisoners at once and to appeal through the local press for support, as there were already several men to whom Mrs. Milne-Redhead had been sending food parcels privately, and which it was known had been received.*

The response was good, and money began to come in. The packing was done every week at Mrs. Milne-Redhead's [sic] house, and the parcels were dispatched from Trudoxhill post office. The number of prisoners increased, and it became a difficult task single-handed, and in October an offer from the committee of the newly formed War Hospital depot in Frome to pack in a room at the depot each week was accepted. The committee most kindly considered in this way the prisoners fund would be better known and supported – this was undoubtedly the case. One was kept busy writing letters of appeal, and every two weeks reports of gifts given and, if possible, the local papers published a letter from a prisoner of war. By this means the fund was more widely known, and regular supplies began to come in. The number of prisoners went up by leaps and bounds, and more packers had to be found. However, though it was no easy task finding the money, perseverance won the day, and the Frome fund has never been short of money and never had to borrow money, and never asked help from the central Prisoners of War Fund, and is now able to hand over between £300 and £400 balance to help start a good club for sailors and soldiers in Frome, which all the prisoners served by the Frome fund are able to use free.

In December 1916, the Central Prisoners of War Fund gave the fund its authorization, and a large committee was formed, Earl Cairns became the chairman, packing days were fixed (six every 4 weeks), and latterly all parcels were 10-11lbs weight, and each cost 10s each.

As the fund was local, the workers packed for men in different regiments. This entailed a lot more work, as permissions from each regiment had to be obtained by form B before the Frome fund could take a prisoner entirely over, and then monthly reports were required to be sent to the regimental associations. Altogether the fund had 84 men through their books, and were packing for 22 when the armistice was signed.

Every Government rule was strictly adhered to, and inspectors came down from London to see all was in order from time to time.

Altogether 5,989 parcels left Frome for Germany, and quite 80 per cent, were safely received and acknowledged. There was a thorough system of checking the parcels, and hundreds of cards were received from the prisoners. Every week each prisoner had a cheery post card with scraps of any home or village news on it to cheer him, and every now and then a letter.

Since Christmas the Frome Fund has entertained all the prisoners to "welcome home" dinners, and each man had a present of tobacco and a service knife as a souvenir of our little fund. A loyal telegram was sent to the King from the prisoners, and a most gracious reply received from him, in which His Majesty thanked the Frome prisoners of war for their loyal message and wished them all a Happy new Year.'

There were also numerous reports in the *Standard* throughout the period of the war documenting various donations and money-raising activities by local communities and groups for the Frome PoW fund. One such donation was made by the Holy Trinity Scouts and Guides. In a news article dated 8 October 1915, the newspaper reported:

'The scouts marched to Mrs. Milne-Redhead under the command of the Rev. E.A. Aust, and delivered the amount of £18.3.6d they had collected on behalf of the "Local prisoners of war fund". Mrs. Milne-Redhead kindly entertained the boys to tea, after which a happy time was spent playing football in the gardens. The boys for their part showed their appreciation by giving vent to three hearty cheers before their departure.'

Letters from prisoners were always well received by the fund, showing them their efforts were appreciated and many were published in the *Standard*. One of the prisoners who wrote was a Sergeant H. Symons of the South Staffordshire Regiment, who had been wounded and then captured in October 1914 during the defence of Calais. A letter to the fund a year into his incarceration showed his appreciation of the organisation's work.

> *'Dear Madam. I wish to thank you and all contributors to your fund on behalf of the other men and myself. When I come home I will be able to thank you all personally, and also explain how welcome your parcels were to us men as prisoners of war…. . I look after the issue of parcels – as you are sending them now stitched up is the best way to send them…. . I will now close; again thanking you for the interest you take in myself and others, and a last thanks to the people of Frome, one and all.'*

Sergeant Symons no doubt got the chance to give his thanks personally, as by April 1919 all the surviving prisoners who had received parcels had been repatriated.

One prisoner of war who sadly did not make it back to Frome was 28-year-old Second Lieutenant Archibald Larcombe of Butts Hill. Before the war he had been the assistant works manager at Butler & Tanner. In early 1916 he left for the Officer Training Corps and qualified for a commission to the Duke of Wellington's (West Riding Regiment) later that year. He arrived on the Western Front in January 1917 and was involved in several heavy engagements, but was taken prisoner after one particular battle in May. According to David L. Adams, in his book *Frome's Fallen Heroes*, Larcombe spent time in a number of German PoW camps *'before being admitted to hospital from a camp at Bad-Coburg, suffering from*

Second Lieutenant Larcombe.

the effects of exposure and deprivation'. He died, still a PoW, around two weeks before the end of the war and is buried near his camp in Niederzwehren Cemetery, Kassel.

There were numerous events, celebrations and services in the days, weeks and months after the Armistice, the first one being, of course, Armistice Day itself. In Frome, once confirmation of the war's end had been given, the town centre quickly became adorned with flags and bunting. Notices for a hastily arranged service of thanksgiving for the cessation of fighting, to be held that evening in the Market Place, were pasted on walls and buildings and the singing of the National Anthem by the large crowd already assembled there was shortly followed by a spontaneously put together band of thirty or so youngsters – with drums, tambourines, cymbals, kazoos and such-like – who paraded through the streets. By the time of the thanksgiving service at six o'clock that evening, 1,500 revellers were packed into the small enclosed area.

Another momentous date, in terms of Frome and the First World War, was 28 June 1919. On this day it was announced that the long-awaited peace treaty had finally been signed in Versailles. As it had

Crowds gather in the Market Place on Peace Day.

A procession going up Bath Street on its way to a service for Peace Day.

been on Armistice Day, crowds of people had already started to gather in the Market Place long before Chairman of the Urban District Council, Mr Woodland, was driven into the centre to deliver the news. To celebrate the signing, the bells of St John's Church were rung and the town's fire siren was sounded. The large crowd then made their way up to Victoria Park where the celebrations continued until late into the evening.

Following swiftly on the heels of the peace treaty celebrations, came the Victory Parade, an event it is said has never been surpassed in the town since, despite the heavy rain that accompanied it. The event took place on Saturday, 19 July 1919, underneath a sea of banners, flags and bunting. The Frome Town Military Band led the procession along Bridge Street and into the Market Place, to the sound of rapturous cheering from the assembled crowd. Behind them came a German gun, pulled by a group of sailors, which had been captured on the Western Front by Royal Field Artillerymen who had completed their training in Frome. This was followed by several other bands and a vast array of school children, ex-servicemen – soldiers, sailors and colonials –

members of various organisations, including the church, councils, fire brigade and nurses, along with carnival-type floats, people in fancy dress and members of the public. Again, celebrations carried on at Victoria Park, although due to persistent downpours several planned events in fact took place the next Thursday (which as it turned out was accompanied by much better weather).

Throughout the war and afterwards, many individuals and organisations were recognised for their contribution towards the war effort. In 1919, however, the town of Frome itself was acknowledged for the financial assistance it had provided towards the treasury's war funds. It was estimated that the people of Frome had donated more than half a million pounds through the Frome War Savings Committee during the war years. In recognition of this fact and to show its appreciation, the Army Council presented the town with a tank. It was a Mark IV (female) Tank No. 231 which, as well as seeing action in France, had recently taken part in a Lord Mayor's show in London.

The tank duly arrived in the town near the end of 1919. It had come by rail, but made the journey to the handing over ceremony at the Recreation Ground under its own power. Before presenting the tank,

The Victory Parade. An event never surpassed in the town before or since.

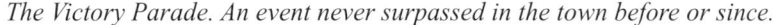

The ceremony handing over the First World War tank to the town of Frome.

Lieutenant McNab, who had driven it from the station, said in his speech that after having been in such murderous and bloody action, he hoped the tank would now stand in 'the green and peaceful fields of Frome'. In the end, it enjoyed these 'peaceful fields' for nearly twenty years before being deemed an eyesore and sold off to the highest bidder, which turned out to be William G. Walter (Bath) Limited.

One individual who deserves a special mention is Captain Arthur Batten-Pooll, recipient of both the Victoria Cross and the Military Cross, as well as being part of that quartet of men whose story is, in many ways, an embodiment perhaps of all of the men who left Frome to go and fight in the Great War.

As mentioned earlier in this book, in January 1915 the *Somerset Standard* published an account of a chance meeting that had occurred a couple of weeks earlier at a French railway station. As well as Captain Batten-Pooll, it involved Corporals Bailey, Long and Sweet. On seeing a trainload of soldiers arrive, Corporal Bailey had called out to see if there was anyone from Frome on board. A trio of local men – Long, Sweet and Batten-Pooll – made themselves known and the four men had shared a meal before bidding farewell.

Service Medals (l to r) the 1914 Star, the British War Medal and the Victory Medal.

What fate befell the four men throughout the war and afterwards? Here are their stories, taking the instigator of the encounter first.

Corporal William Bailey survived the war and received the 1914/15 Star, the British War Medal and also the Victory Medal. He returned to Frome and resumed his job as trainer for Frome Town Football Club. Corporal Arthur Long, however, sadly did not make it back to civilian life. He was killed in action six months after the chance meeting; a shell exploding in the trench he was in the process of building up, causing instant death. Like Corporal Bailey though, Corporal Willoughby Sweet survived the war and received the 1914/15 Star, along with both the British War and Victory medals. The final member of this quartet, however, had the most distinguished career of them all.

Captain Arthur Batten-Pooll was the youngest son of Captain R.P.H Batten-Pooll and Mrs Sophia Batten-Pooll of Rode Manor. His mother was a known Suffragette sympathiser and their Rode home was frequently filled with high profile Suffragettes prior to the war. In 1913

Mrs Batten-Pooll had employed Mrs Pankhurst's daughter Adela to work at the Manor and two days before the war began had waited outside the Bath courts, with her car engine running, ready to whisk Gertrude Francis, there on a charge of arson, safely away after she had been bailed. Once the war broke out though, all campaigning by Suffragettes came to a halt, so as to concentrate on the war effort.

As for Captain Arthur Batten-Pooll, he showed he had obviously inherited the same fighting spirit as his mother. In June 1916, while in command of a raiding party on the Western Front, a bomb had exploded near Captain Batten-Pooll, mutilating all the fingers of his right hand; despite this, he continued to give orders and direct operations. He was wounded twice more, while trying to rescue others, then collapsed on his return to the British lines. He was awarded the Victoria Cross 'for most conspicuous bravery' and received his medal from King George V in November of that year. As stated previously, he was awarded the

Arthur Batten-Pooll,

Rode Manor, residence of the Batten-Pooll family.

Military Cross for gallantry during an action the following year.

In November 1917, during the Third Battle of Ypres (Passchendaele), he went missing in action. For several weeks he was presumed to have been killed, as the last sighting saw him surrounded by Germans and fighting desperately with a handful of fellow men to hold the position. Towards the end of December, however, it was announced he was a prisoner of war, his capture being the outcome of that last engagement with the enemy. He eventually returned to Frome a war hero and died in 1971.

There were many changes to the home front brought about by the First World War, but perhaps one of the most significant was the way in which the pre-war perception of a woman's role in society was challenged and successfully

The Victoria Cross, the highest military award for valor.

altered. Women had shown themselves capable of taking on jobs traditionally the reserve of men and doing them admirably. One example, of course, being the women employed in munitions work for J.W. Singer & Sons. Although the returning men would, in the majority of cases, resume their former occupations, women's movement groups – mainly the Suffragettes – now had proof of their capability, attained in the years the men were away, which could not be denied. Ultimately this led to women getting the vote and the first election they were able to participate in – at least those that were eligible – occurred on Saturday, 14 December 1918.

The election of December 1918 provided somewhat of a shock result. Sir John Barlow, who had been Frome's Member of Parliament for the previous twenty-two years, was sensationally ousted from his seat. In retrospect, it is perhaps not too much of a surprise; he had, after all, voted against the parliamentary bill introducing conscription, had sent his son away to America during the war, and his Quaker pacifist beliefs were perhaps at odds with a town still celebrating the war's end but remembering those who had died. His successor was the

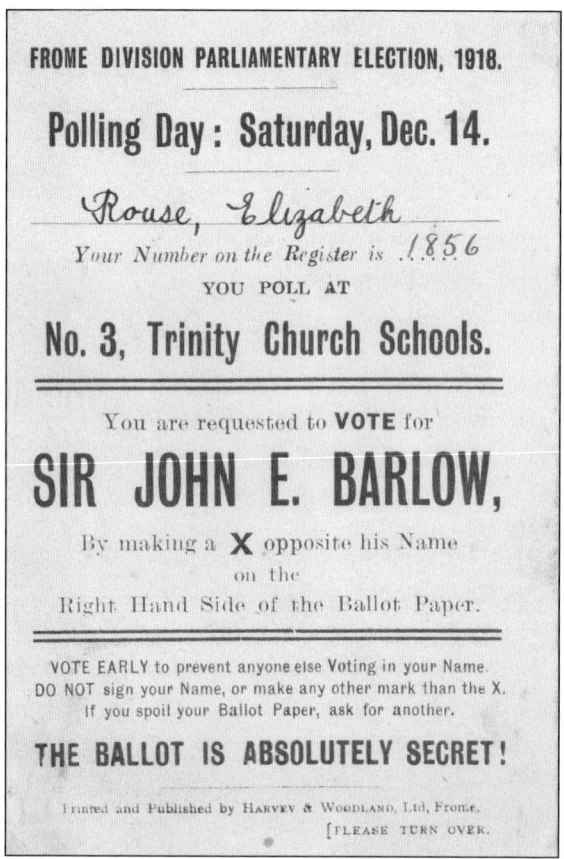

FROME DIVISION PARLIAMENTARY ELECTION, 1918.

Polling Day : Saturday, Dec. 14.

Rouse, Elizabeth

Your Number on the Register is *1856*

YOU POLL AT

No. 3, Trinity Church Schools.

You are requested to **VOTE** for

SIR JOHN E. BARLOW,

By making a **X** opposite his Name

on the

Right Hand Side of the Ballot Paper.

VOTE EARLY to prevent anyone else Voting in your Name.
DO NOT sign your Name, or make any other mark than the X.
If you spoil your Ballot Paper, ask for another.

THE BALLOT IS ABSOLUTELY SECRET!

Printed and Published by HARVEY & WOODLAND, Ltd, Frome.

[PLEASE TURN OVER.

Polling Card for the Frome Division Parliamentary Election in December 1918.

Conservative candidate Percy Hurd, grandfather of future Home Secretary Douglas Hurd.

When Mr Woodland, Frome Urban District Council Chairman, announced the news of the Versailles Peace Treaty signing, in June 1919, he also gave a sobering reminder to those becoming intoxicated through their rejoicing. He said that while doing so, they should not forget that hundreds of thousands of their fellow countrymen had given their lives for Britain, and that thousands of homes were mourning the loss of their loved ones that day. In the Frome area, these households would include the Stillmans, Millers, Hanneys, Hobbs, Hilliers, Whites, Crooks, and Wheelers, and too many more families to list in this limited space. And yet, in spite of the fighting having been over for more than eight months, these mourning families were still being joined by others. The Dix family, for instance, had lost their son, Herbert, a former private in the Bedfordshire Regiment, a few months prior to Mr Woodland's speech, while Private Charles Baily's family suffered his death less than a week after it.

And still the returning soldiers died and not all from influenza; in fact, according to the book *Frome's Fallen Heroes: The Great War*, the last death the author includes is that of Bandsman William Pothecary, who according to the CWGC, died of his

What Sir John Barlow stands for.

A Peace of Justice,

A League of Nations,

Limitation of Armaments,

Abolition of Conscription,

Quick Return of Soldiers to Civil Life,

A Higher Minimum Standard of Life,

Justice to Ireland.

Maintenance of Free Trade,

Equal Opportunity in Education,

Drastic Land and Housing Programme,

Liberal Pensions for Soldiers and Dependents who have suffered through the War.

VOTE FOR BARLOW!

Despite his best efforts, John Barlow lost his seat.

Christ Church where many graves of those killed in the First World War are located.

wounds on 20 June 1921. This was almost two years to the day of that poignant address.

It is sometimes easy to forget, reading David L. Adams' book, that the majority of the privates, corporals, sergeants, bandsmen, able seamen, stokers, gunners and all the other ranks recorded, held, prior to the war, civilian jobs. This is possibly one of the greatest consequences of that conflict, in so much as not only did individual families in Frome and the surrounding villages, such as Mells, Rode, Beckington, Nunney, Buckland Dinham and Orchardleigh, to name a few, lose their sons, husbands, fathers, nephews, uncles, grandsons and perhaps even grandfathers and great-grandfathers, but the communities as a whole lost an integral part of themselves. These men who went off to fight, never to return, had acquired numbers, ranks and regimental badges to do so, yet before that fateful day in August 1914, they had been the milkmen, postmen, grocers, butchers, fishmongers, bakers, printers, electricians, plumbers, draughtsmen, fitters, solicitors, teachers, drivers, painters, architects, coachmen, gardeners, draymen, labourers, clergymen, miners, florists, booksellers, porters, wheelwrights, colliers, saddlers, drapers and all the other occupations that are at the heart of any hamlet, parish, village or town.

All these vacant roles would, in time, have more than likely been filled once more and the communities continued to function normally. But no matter how easy or difficult it was to employ someone else to do these jobs, the void their predecessors had left in the fabric of these close knit communities, through their untimely deaths, could never be eradicated and would never be forgotten.

Afterword

Throughout the centenary years of the First World War the town of Frome and the villages surrounding it have been holding services and ceremonies to mark the events that happened during the period 1914-1918. At the same time, they have been remembering those from their communities who answered the call of King and Country, along with those who contributed to the war effort at home.

For those who did not return, having been killed in the various theatres of war around the world, the memorials, honour rolls, statues and gravestones erected in post war years became a special focus of attention. Possibly the most poignant event in Frome during these centennial occasions though, took place on the day before the actual anniversary of the outbreak of the First World War. On this day, Sunday, 3 August 2014, a statue based on a former soldier was unveiled outside the Frome Memorial Theatre, situated on Christchurch Street West.

A remembrance service for Victoria Cross recipient, Wilfred Dolby Fuller, took place at Christ Church, Frome, to mark the centenary of the action in which the medal was awarded.

Flyer for the Dedication Service.

The story behind this ceremony is a remarkable and fascinating one in itself and begins in the aftermath of the First World War. After hostilities had ended, J.W. Singer & Sons ceased being a munitions manufacturer and reverted back to its former role. With the demand that sprang up around the world for statues, figures, friezes, wreaths and tablets for memorials to commemorate the fallen, many returning soldiers who resumed their jobs at Singer's factory, found they were involved in creating lasting memorials to their own dead comrades.

In Frome, several permanent memorials were planned to commemorate the fallen; one of these being the Frome Memorial Theatre, originally Memorial Hall, which was completed in 1925. Inside the foyer, a roll of honour lists the names of many of the Frome men who gave the ultimate sacrifice. Three years earlier, in 1922, a statue of a soldier was ordered and someone was needed to 'model' it. For some reason, now lost in time, Charlie Robbins was selected.

Frome Museum held a major exhibition on the First World War in 2014 to commemorate the centenary of its start.

The Memorial Stone was laid in September 1924.

The centrepiece of the memorial inside the theatre.

Charlie Robbins, along with his brother James, worked at J.W. Singer & Sons before the war and both enlisted in August 1914, Charlie serving with the 2nd/5th Battalion of the Gloucester Regiment. Starting off as a lance corporal, he was later promoted to sergeant. Although the brothers experienced their share of heavy fighting, they survived the war and came back to work at Singer's. Charlie married, lived the rest of his life in Frome and died in 1981.

'Charlie Robbins'.

Once the statue had been completed, however, the person who ordered it had run out of money and so 'Charlie' was put away in a storeroom where he lay undisturbed for several decades. When he was 'rediscovered', in the early 1970s, he was 'dusted down' and given pride of place outside the firm's offices.

The statue was moved again in 1999, when J.W. Singer & Sons was bought by another company, Tyco, but once more put in a prominent place outside of their premises on the Marston Trading Estate in the town. Here it stayed for the next fifteen years 'welcoming' staff and visitors alike. During this period of time, however, there were various attempts at getting 'Charlie' moved to a more prominent public location, where the community as a whole could benefit from seeing him, one of these locations being outside the Frome Memorial Theatre. To coincide with the First World War centenary, Tyco finally agreed to a permanent loan of the statue, so it could be situated outside this building.

In echoes of the community spirit which had carried Frome through the First World War, an army of volunteers set about preparing the site, laying several tons of stones and slabs over six weeks. At the same

The Memorial Theatre in Frome: the town's official memorial to all those who fell in the First World War.

time, businesses, the town council, Frome Museum and many other individuals and organisations donated their time, expertise and materials, as they all worked together to implement this long-held dream. With everything in place, the statue was moved from Tyco to its new site in late July 2014, ready for the unveiling ceremony a few days later, when it would become Frome's official memorial to the fallen of the town. The entire process was captured on film by the Frome Film and Video Makers Club, who eventually released the DVD 'Welcome Home Charlie Robbins'.

The undertaking of this memorial project, perhaps above all, epitomises once more the special character of Frome, which has existed ever since its foundation more than 1300 years ago, and the sense of community that came together for the greater good a hundred years ago. The people of present-day Frome, then, with every stone that was placed and every slab that was laid, echoing and honouring the spirit of those predecessors who gave so much, yet ultimately achieved their aim: that of victory and continued freedom for themselves, their families and their decendants to go about our everyday lives.

Select Bibliography

ADAMS, David L., Frome's Fallen Heroes: The Great War
ARTHUR, Max, Symbol of Courage
BELHAM, Peter, The Making of Frome
BLANNING, William, In the Company of Heroes
GILL, Derek, Britain in Old Photographs: Frome; Frome School
  Days
GILLARD, Brian, Good Old Somersets
GOODALL, Rodney, The Buildings of Frome
LANGFORD, William, The Great War Illustrated: 1914
McGARVIE, Michael, The Book of Frome; Frome in Old Postcards
  Vols 1 & 2

Other sources:
Frome Standard
Somerset Standard
Somerset and Wiltshire Journal

Index